hamlyn
Quick**Cook**

hamlyn

QuickCook
Family Meals

Recipes by Emma Jane Frost

Every dish, three ways – you choose!
30 minutes | 20 minutes | 10 minutes

An Hachette UK company
www.hachette.co.uk

First published in Great Britain in 2012 by Hamlyn,
a division of Octopus Publishing Group Ltd
Endeavour House, 189 Shaftesbury Avenue, London WC2H 8JY
www.octopusbooks.co.uk

Recipes by Emma Jane Frost
Copyright © Octopus Publishing Group Ltd 2012

ISBN: 978-0-60062-359-5

A CIP catalogue record for this book is available from the British Library

Printed and bound in China

1 2 3 4 5 6 7 8 9 10

Both metric and imperial measurements are given for the recipes.
Use one set of measurements only, not a mixture of both.

Standard level spoon measurements are used in all recipes
1 tablespoon = 15 ml
1 teaspoon = 5 ml

Ovens should be preheated to the specified temperature. If using a fan-assisted
oven, follow the manufacturer's instructions for adjusting the time and temperature.

Eggs should be medium unless otherwise stated. The Department of Health advises
that eggs should not be consumed raw. This book contains some dishes made with
raw or lightly cooked eggs. It is prudent for more vulnerable people, such as pregnant
and nursing mothers, invalids, the elderly, babies and young children, to avoid
uncooked or lightly cooked dishes made with eggs.

This book includes dishes made with nuts and nut derivatives. It is advisable for those
with known allergic reactions to nuts and nut derivatives and those who may be
potentially vulnerable to these allergies, such as pregnant and nursing mothers,
invalids, the elderly, babies and children, to avoid dishes made with nuts and nut oils.
It is also prudent to check the labels of prepared ingredients for the possible inclusion
of nut derivatives.

Contents

Introduction

30 20 10 – quick, quicker, quickest

This book offers a new and flexible approach to meal-planning for busy cooks and lets you choose the recipe option that best fits the time you have available. Inside you will find 360 dishes that will inspire you and motivate you to get cooking every day of the year. All the recipes take a maximum of 30 minutes to cook. Some take as little as 20 minutes and, amazingly, many take only 10 minutes. With a bit of preparation, you can easily try out one new recipe from this book each night and slowly you will build a wide and exciting portfolio of recipes to suit your needs.

How Does It Work?

Every recipe in the QuickCook series can be cooked one of three ways – a 30-minute version, a 20-minute version or a super-quick and easy 10-minute version. At the beginning of each chapter you'll find recipes listed by time. Choose a dish based on how much time you have and turn to that page.

You'll find the main recipe in the middle of the page with a beautiful photograph and two time-variations below.

If you enjoy the dish, you can go back and cook the other time options. If you liked the 30-minute Smoky Chicken and Prawn Paella, but only have 10 minutes to spare, then you'll find a way to cook it using cheat ingredients or clever shortcuts.

If you love the ingredients and flavours of the 10-minute Mango and Spinach Salad with Warm Peanut Chicken, why not try something more substantial like the 20-minute Chicken and Mango Kebabs, or be inspired to cook a more elaborate version like a Chicken Stir-Fry with Mango and Peanut Sauce. Alternatively, browse through all of the 360 delicious recipes, find something that takes your eye – then cook the version that fits your time frame.

Or, for easy inspiration, turn to the gallery on pages 12–19 to get an instant overview by themes, such as Winter Warmers or Weekend Treats.

QuickCook online

To make life even easier, you can use the special code on each recipe page to email yourself a recipe card for printing, or email a text-only shopping list to your phone. Go to www.hamlynquickcook.com and enter the recipe code at the bottom of each page.

FAM-MEAT-DYQ

QuickCook Family Meals

In today's modern society, there is a great amount of pressure on a family's time. Parents tend to work, children have more and more extra-curricular activities and generally, life is packed to the gills with activity and busyness. It is not a surprise then that supermarket ready-meals have risen so dramatically in popularity over the last decade. How many times have we got home at the end of a busy day to find ourselves looking into an uninspiring fridge and wondering what on earth we are going to feed everyone? It is too easy to pop a cheap ready-meal into the microwave or call for an expensive, fat-filled takeaway. But our message to you in this book is that you can cook a really tasty, fabulous-looking family supper with limited ingredients, quickly and easily.

You've heard it said about DIY, but it is also true of cookery. Fail to prepare and you prepare to fail! Whether you are an experienced cook or a complete novice, if you don't have a quick think in the morning before work about what meal you're going to be rustling up for your family that evening, come 6 o'clock you'll be spending unnecessary amounts of time defrosting food and nipping to the corner shop for missing ingredients. Much as it sounds obvious, do take a few minutes to plan in the morning, and get fish or meat out of the freezer ready, and make a quick shopping list so you can get whatever you need when you're out that day.

The Art of Multi-Tasking

The best chefs in the world are the ones who can be cooking 20 things at once whilst keeping calm and in control! We are not asking you to cook 20 things at once, but we do suggest you learn the great art of multi -tasking in the kitchen. For instance, our Apricot-Glazed Gammon Steaks with Paprika Potatoes on page 92 require you to put the potatoes on to boil at the beginning, then whilst they are cooking, to start pan-cooking the other ingredients. Whilst you are making the sauce, you have to go back to finish off the potatoes and then the whole meal comes together at roughly the same time. Without a bit of juggling with your hob, grill and oven, it will be impossible to muster up a meal in 30 minutes or less, but follow our recipes in the order they say and you'll be pleasantly surprised at how quickly supper comes together.

The Right Tools for the Job

With the right ingredients in stock, the art of multi-tasking mastered and motivation levels high, the only thing left to consider are the tools at hand. Do not underestimate how vitally important good tools are to help make the cooking process not just easier but a lot more enjoyable. The first and most important tool is a large, heavy-based frying pan. Without one of these many of our recipes will be tricky to master. A thick, heavy base to your pan gives a more even temperature spread and can therefore prevent burning.

Knives are also vital to get right. A knife that is regularly sharpened can work four or five times quicker than a blunt one. Likewise, a can opener that works first time will save minutes and will keep stress levels at a minimum! A grater that you can hold comfortably, has many slicing options and most importantly, that is sharp, will feel like a help rather than a hindrance. And we highly recommend buying yourself a good-quality food processor; whizzing up pastes and soups and chopping fruits and nuts will suddenly seem as easy as pie and you will wonder why on earth you didn't buy one before!

Easy Ingredients

There are a whole array of tasty, wonderful foods that lend themselves to fast, tasty, nutritious suppers.

Eggs, for a start, are a smart choice for a busy cook, being hugely versatile and taking a few minutes to cook. The key is to buy well – organic or farm-bought eggs really do tend to have a greater intensity of flavour and a richer colour – and to blend them with exciting ingredients that will give them a whole new lease of life. Check out our Feta, Pepper and Cherry Tomato Frittata on page 24 or the Bacon, Onion and Egg Pan-Cooked Tart on page 90 for new ways with eggs.

Noodles are another super-easy food that are ludicrously fast to cook and can be added to soups or stir-fries after only 3 or 4 minutes cooking. Like eggs, the key is to add plenty of 'easy' flavour. Coconut milk and fresh coriander are wonderful in Thai-style soups, and garlic, chillies, ginger, Chinese 5-spice and soy sauce are must-haves for successful stir-fries. And when time is really short, why not keep a handful of stir-in sauces in your kitchen cupboard? It may seem like cheating, but surely a freshly prepared soup or stir-fry of wholesome vegetables, noodles and protein with a shop-bought paste or sauce is better for your family than a frozen ready-meal or an expensive, calorie-laden takeaway?

When buying meat such as beef or lamb, be aware when that the cheaper the cut of meat, often the tougher it is and therefore the longer cooking time it needs. Use frying steak or lamb cutlets, chicken breast or boneless thighs, and when buying pork, choose thin cuts with little or no fat. Cut all the meat you use really thinly so it cooks through quickly and easily without becoming tough in the pan.

When time allows, it is always advisable to feed your family wholegrains and wholemeal versions of their usual favourite carbs. However, do be aware that brown rice can take up to 30 minutes to cook and brown pasta always takes a little longer to cook than white pasta. We suggest buying 'easy cook' versions of wholefoods wherever possible, and to speed up the process of cooking pasta and rice, use kettle-boiled water. Don't try and heat cold water on the hob – you will add a good 5 minutes to your overall cooking time!

Lastly, don't feel afraid to go to the preserved vegetables section in the supermarket and stock up on jars of chargrilled artichokes, olives, roasted tomatoes, stuffed peppers and other interesting vegetables in flavoured oils. Adding these to pasta, rice and salads are a guaranteed easy way of adding flavour, colour and interest to your family's supper.

Easy Flavour
Many stews, roasts and bakes infuse and develop their flavours through their long cooking times but at the end of a busy day, you don't have 2 or 3 hours to cook supper. Therefore to create the same intensity of flavours when cooking meals in a quarter of the usual cooking time, you need to ensure you use 'easy flavour'. By this we mean foods that give intense and almost instant taste. So stock your cupboards with garlic paste (usually found alongside tomato purée in the supermarket), ready-chopped fresh ginger and lemon grass purée; a good selection of dried herbs and spices; soy sauce; coconut milk; different types of mustards; Tabasco sauce; stock cubes and preserved lemon juice. In your fridge, it cannot hurt to keep in some tasty, preserved meats such as chorizo and Parma ham alongside fresh onions, fresh garlic, reduced-fat feta cheese and all your favourite colourful, crunchy vegetables.

Winter Warmers

Welcoming recipes for cold winter days.

Pea, Mint and Bacon Soup with Crème Fraîche 26

Mushroom and Thyme Soup with Goats' Cheese Croûtes 38

Cauliflower Cheese Soup 56

One-Pan Chicken with Honeyed Roots and Stuffing 78

Tray-Baked Sausages with Apples and Onions 86

Turkey Meatballs in Rich Tomato and Herb Sauce 114

Mixed Mushroom Stroganoff 194

Tomato, Rosemary and Cannellini Bean Stew 200

Penne with Pan-Fried Butternut Squash and Pesto 204

Raspberry Rice Brûlée 240

Pear and Chocolate Crumble 238

Treacle Sponge Microwave Puddings 264

One of Your 5-a-Day

Tasty meals using seasonal fruit and vegetables.

**Aubergine and Garlic Dip
with Toasted Pitta** 52

Thai Vegetable Curry 182

**Fruity Chickpea Tagine
with Coriander Couscous** 208

**Warm Spiced Plums
with Ice Cream** 244

**Mango and Spinach Salad
with Warm Peanut Chicken** 72

**Lemon Mixed Vegetable
Kebabs with Nut Pilaff** 192

**Vegetable, Fruit and Nut
Biryani** 212

**Rhubarb and Ginger
Tartlets** 258

**Lamb and Tray-Roasted
Vegetables with Chickpeas** 112

**Goats' Cheese and
Spinach Risotto** 198

**Butternut Squash, Tomato
and Red Onion Gratin** 222

**Griddled Madeira Cake
with Fruit Compote** 262

Weekend Treats

Delicious recipes to indulge you and your family.

Salami and Sweetcorn Hash with Poached Eggs 36

Fried Eggy Bread Sandwich with Mozzarella 48

Sweetcorn Fritters with Chilli and Tomato Salsa 50

Eggs Florentine 54

Fillet of Beef with a Mustard Crust and Oven Chips 74

Apricot-Glazed Gammon Steaks with Paprika Potatoes 92

Roasted Smoked Haddock with Mash and Poached Eggs 170

Spicy Bean Burgers with Tomato Salsa 184

Coconut Dahl with Toasted Naan Fingers 224

Chocolate and Raspberry Layers 234

Make-Ahead Cheesecakes with Berry Compote 236

Chocolate Mousse with Pistachio Ice Cream 250

Healthy Midweek Meals

Great-tasting low-fat meals everyone will enjoy.

Thai Chicken Soup 46

Chargrilled Chicken with
Salsa and Fruity Couscous 64

Sweet and Sour Pork with
Fresh Pineapple Chunks 66

Asian-Style Beef Skewers
with Satay Sauce 110

Poached Chicken with
Thai Red Curry Sauce 124

Creamy Scallops
with Leeks 144

Lemony Prawns and
Broccoli Stir-Fry 154

Cherry Tomato and
Cod Stir-Fry with Bacon 172

Sticky Honey and Chilli Salmon
Skewers with Rice 174

Egg, Basil and Cheese Salad
with Cherry Tomatoes 188

Puy Lentil Stew with Garlic
and Herb Bread 226

Oat-Topped Orchard Fruit
Crumbles 254

Kids' Favourites

Always a winner with the little ones.

Creamy Ham and Mustard Pasta 42

Artichoke, Olive and Taleggio Mini Pizzas 58

Sausage, Rosemary and Mixed Bean Hotpot 70

Mushroom and Cheese Burgers with Cucumber Salsa 98

Crispy Cod Goujons with Lime and Caper Mayonnaise 136

Tuna Pasta Gratin with Butternut Squash and Peas 142

Pan-Fried Cod and Chips with Lemon Mayo and Dill 160

Cheesy Tuna and Sweetcorn Fishcakes 164

Roasted Vegetable Pasta with Garlic and Herb Sauce 186

Banoffee Layers 252

Chocolate Puddle Pudding 266

Caramel Bananas 276

Straight From The Pan

Try something new with these one-pot wonders.

Feta, Pepper and Cherry Tomato Frittata 24

Coconut Soup with Spinach and Butternut Squash 34

Special Fried Rice 84

Bacon, Onion and Egg Pan-Cooked Tart 90

Rustic Lamb and Potato Curry 96

Smoky Chicken and Prawn Paella 106

Sticky Gammon Steaks with Caramelized Onions 118

Salmon with Green Vegetables 132

Cajun Spiced Salmon Frittata with Peppers 166

Chunky Vegetable Red Lentil Dahl 216

Cauliflower and Potato Curry with Spinach 220

Coconut Dahl with Toasted Naan Fingers 224

Special Occasions

For when the family deserve something special.

**Chicken Thighs with Lemon
Crème Fraîche and Greens** 88

**Coq au Vin-Style Chicken
Breasts** 94

**Stir-Fried Duck with Sugar
Snaps and Orange Rice** 102

**Lamb Fillet with Mushroom
and Spinach Sauce** 104

**Pork Escalopes
with Prosciutto** 116

**Parma Ham and Pesto-
Wrapped Monkfish** 138

Creamy Haddock Gratin 150

**Black Olive and Sunblush
Tomato Risotto with Cod** 176

**Spinach, Pine Nut
and Cheese Filo Pie** 210

**White Chocolate Cream
with Raspberries** 242

Caramel Pear Tart Tatin 268

**Quick Tiramisu
with Strawberries** 278

Taste of Summer

Recipes packed with the fresh flavours of summer.

Crisp-Fried Citrusy Calamari with Chilli Sauce 40

Brie, Pepper and Spinach Deep-Set Frittata 44

Chicken and Tarragon Burgers 68

Chicken and Chorizo Jambalaya with Peppers 76

Spicy Cajun Chicken Quinoa with Dried Apricots 100

Parmesan-Crusted Haddock with Tomato Avocado Salsa 130

Jamaican Spiced Salmon with Corn and Okra 156

Garlic and Tomato Seafood Spaghetti 162

Grilled Haloumi with Warm Couscous Salad 202

Apricots with Lemon Cream and Soft Amaretti 246

Pan-Fried Pineapple with Rum and Raisins 256

Scone, Strawberry Jam and Clotted Cream Trifles 270

QuickCook

Snacks, Starters and Light Bites

Recipes listed by cooking time

10

2 Feta, Pepper and Cherry Tomato Frittata

Serves 4

3 tablespoons olive oil
1 red pepper, cored, deseeded
    and cut into chunks
1 red onion, roughly chopped
175 g (6 oz) cherry tomatoes,
    halved
6 eggs
200 g (7 oz) feta cheese, drained
    and crumbled
handful of rocket leaves
salt and pepper

- Heat 2 tablespoons of the oil in a 23 cm (9 inch) nonstick frying pan and cook the red pepper and onion over a medium heat, stirring occasionally, for 5 minutes until softened. Add the tomatoes and cook, stirring, for 2 minutes.

- Beat the eggs in a bowl and season with plenty of salt and pepper, then pour over the vegetable mixture in the pan. Scatter over the feta and cook over a low heat for 4–5 minutes until the base of the frittata is set.

- Place the pan under a preheated medium grill, making sure that the pan handle is turned away from the heat, and cook for 3–4 minutes until the top is golden and set. Remove from the grill, scatter the rocket over the centre of the frittata and season with a good grinding of pepper. Drizzle with the remaining tablespoon of oil and serve cut into wedges.

1 Feta, Pepper and Cherry Tomato Salad

Toss together 1 red pepper, cored, deseeded and cut into chunks, 1 chopped red onion, 175 g (6 oz) halved cherry tomatoes and 200 g (7 oz) crumbled feta cheese in a bowl with 100 g (3½ oz) pitted black olives and 75 g (3 oz) rocket leaves. Whisk together the juice of 1 lemon, 4 tablespoons olive oil and 2 tablespoons chopped parsley in a small jug, and toss with the salad before serving.

3 Sausage, Pepper and Cherry Tomato Frittata

Heat 1 tablespoon olive oil in a 23 cm (9 inch) nonstick frying pan and cook 4 chorizo-style pork sausages over a medium heat, turning frequently, for 8–10 minutes until browned all over and cooked through. Remove and thickly slice. Heat 2 tablespoons olive oil in the pan and cook 1 red pepper, cored, deseeded and cut into chunks, and 1 chopped red onion over a medium heat, stirring occasionally, for 5 minutes.

Add the sliced sausages and 175 g (6 oz) halved cherry tomatoes and cook, stirring, for 2 minutes. Beat 6 eggs in a bowl and season with plenty of salt and pepper, then pour over the mixture in the pan. Cook over a low heat for 4–5 minutes until the base is set. Place the pan under a preheated medium grill, making sure that the pan handle is turned away from the heat, and cook for 3–4 minutes until the top is golden and set.

3 Pea, Mint and Bacon Soup with Crème Fraîche

Serves 4

2 tablespoons olive oil

1 onion, roughly chopped

6 rindless back bacon rashers, chopped

4 tablespoons chopped mint

250 g (8 oz) peeled potatoes, chopped

500 g (1 lb) frozen peas

1.2 litres (2 pints) chicken stock

4 tablespoons crème fraîche

salt and pepper

roasted mixed seeds, to serve

- Heat the oil in a large, heavy-based saucepan and cook the onion and bacon over a medium heat, stirring frequently, for 5 minutes until the onion is softened and the bacon browned. Add the mint and potatoes and cook, stirring, for 1 minute, then add the peas and stock. Bring to the boil, then reduce the heat, cover and simmer for 15 minutes until the potatoes are tender.

- Transfer the soup in 2 batches to a food processor and whizz until smooth. Return to the pan, swirl in the crème fraîche and heat through for 1 minute.

- Season with a little salt and pepper, then ladle into warmed serving bowls and scatter with roasted seeds to serve.

---

1 Up-Styled Shop-Bought Pea and Mint Soup Warm through 600 ml (1 pint) ready-made fresh pea and mint soup in a saucepan. Meanwhile, chop 100 g (3½ oz) pancetta slices. Heat 1 tablespoon olive oil in a frying pan and cook the pancetta with a handful of torn focaccia bread over a high heat until crisp and golden. Serve the soup ladled into warmed bowls with the pancetta and bread scattered on top.

2 Summer Pea Soup with Feta and Pesto Toasts Heat 2 tablespoons olive oil in a large, heavy-based saucepan and cook 1 chopped onion and 1 chopped garlic clove over a medium heat, stirring frequently, for 5 minutes. Add 500 g (1 lb) frozen petit pois and 1.2 litres (2 pints) chicken stock. Bring to the boil, then simmer for 5 minutes. Transfer in 2 batches to a food processor and whizz until smooth. Return to the pan, stir in 4 tablespoons crème fraîche, season and heat through for 1 minute. Meanwhile, cut 8 slices from a bloomer loaf and toast under a preheated high grill on one side only. Top the untoasted sides with 200 g (7 oz) drained, crumbled feta cheese and dot with 2 tablespoons green pesto. Grill for a further 3 minutes or until golden. Ladle the soup into warmed bowls and serve 2 toasts with each.

30 Roasted Indian Sweet Potato Wedges with Raita

Serves 4

2 teaspoons cumin seeds

2 teaspoons coriander seeds

½ teaspoon fenugreek seeds

2 tablespoons sunflower oil

2 x 300 g (10 oz) packs ready-prepared sweet potato wedges

¼ teaspoon dried chilli flakes

salt and pepper

For the raita

200 ml (7 fl oz) natural Greek yogurt

4 tablespoons chopped mint

¼ cucumber, finely diced

- Place all the spices in a small, heavy-based frying pan and cook over a high heat for 1 minute, swirling the pan to toast the seeds evenly. Transfer to a mortar and grind with a pestle until finely ground. Mix the ground spices with the oil, then toss with the sweet potato wedges in a large bowl.

- Spread the wedges out in a large roasting tin, season with salt and pepper and scatter with the chilli flakes. Place in a preheated oven, 200°C (400°F), Gas Mark 6, for 20 minutes until beginning to brown. Meanwhile, mix together the ingredients for the raita and place in a small serving bowl.

- Remove the roasted sweet potato wedges from the oven and serve with the raita for dipping.

 ### 1 Sweet Potato Crisps

Heat 300 ml (½ pint) vegetable oil in a deep, heavy-based saucepan to 180–190°C (350–375°F), or until a cube of bread browns in 30 seconds. Meanwhile, thinly slice 2 peeled sweet potatoes with a mandolin or vegetable peeler. Deep-fry in small batches for 1–2 minutes until browned. Remove with a slotted spoon and drain on kitchen paper. Sprinkle with sea salt and cumin seeds. Serve with a 190 g (6¾ oz) jar raita and some prepared fresh vegetables cut into chunks for dipping.

 ### 2 Roasted Indian-Style Sweet Potato and Squash

Toss 350 g (11½ oz) ready-prepared diced butternut squash and sweet potato with 2 tablespoons korma curry paste and 2 tablespoons natural yogurt in a large bowl. Spread out in a large roasting tin and place in a preheated oven, 220°C (425°F), Gas Mark 7, for 15 minutes. Meanwhile, make the raita as above and serve alongside the roasted vegetables.

10 Smoked Salmon, Soft Cheese and Chive Omelette

Serves 4

2 tablespoons vegetable oil
6 eggs, beaten
200 g (7 oz) soft cheese
1 tablespoon cold water
100 g (3½ oz) smoked salmon pieces
3 tablespoons snipped chives
salt and pepper
salad, to serve (optional)

- Heat the oil in a large, heavy-based frying pan. Season the eggs with salt and pepper, then pour into the pan and cook over a gentle heat for 4–5 minutes until the base is set and the top is almost set.

- Meanwhile, beat the soft cheese in a bowl with the measurement water until very soft.

- Spoon the cheese over the omelette and gently spread a little. Arrange the smoked salmon over the top, then scatter over the chives and cook gently for a further 1 minute until the top is warm.

- Fold one side of the omelette over the other. Serve cut into 4 wedges, with a simple salad, if liked.

---

20 Smoked Salmon and Chive Mini Soufflés

Soufflés Melt 15 g (½ oz) butter in a saucepan, add 15 g (½ oz) plain flour and cook over a medium heat, stirring, for a few seconds. Remove from the heat and add 150 ml (¼ pint) milk, a little at a time, blending well between each addition. Return to the heat, then bring to the boil, stirring constantly, cooking until thickened. Stir in 50 g (2 oz) roughly chopped smoked salmon, 1 tablespoon finely chopped chives and salt and pepper. Whisk 2 eggs in a grease-free bowl until stiff peaks form, then gently fold into the sauce. Divide between 4 individual ramekins, place on a baking sheet and bake in a preheated oven, 200°C (400°F), Gas Mark 6, for 10 minutes until golden and puffed. Serve immediately.

---

30 Baked Smoked Salmon, Pea and Dill Tortilla Squares

Dill Tortilla Squares Beat 6 eggs in a bowl with 4 tablespoons chopped dill and plenty of pepper. Stir in 100 g (3½ oz) snipped smoked salmon and 100 g (3½ oz) frozen peas, then pour into a lightly greased 20 cm (8 inch) square cake tin. Place in a preheated oven, 200°C (400°F), Gas Mark 6, for 20–25 minutes until browned in places and firm to the touch. Cut into chunky squares to serve.

30 Crispy Chilli Beef with Vegetables

Serves 4

vegetable oil, for deep-frying and stir-frying
2 eggs
2 tablespoons cornflour
300 g (10 oz) frying steak, thinly sliced into strips
2 carrots, peeled and shredded
1 bunch of spring onions, shredded
100 g (3½ oz) sugar snap peas, halved
1 red chilli, sliced
2 tablespoons caster sugar
4 tablespoons rice vinegar
4 tablespoons sweet chilli sauce
1 tablespoon light soy sauce

- Fill a deep, heavy-based saucepan a quarter full with vegetable oil and heat to 180–190°C (350–375°F), or until a cube of bread browns in 30 seconds. Meanwhile, beat together the eggs and cornflour thoroughly in a bowl. Add the beef strips and toss to coat.

- Deep-fry the beef strips in 2 batches, lowering them into the oil with a slotted spoon and cooking for 10 seconds before stirring to prevent the strips from sticking together. Continue to cook for 5 minutes until golden and crisp. Remove with the slotted spoon and drain on kitchen paper.

- Heat 1 tablespoon oil in a large wok or heavy-based frying pan over a high heat and stir-fry the carrots, spring onions, sugar snap peas and chilli for 2–3 minutes until softened. Add the sugar, rice vinegar and sweet chilli and soy sauces, mix well and cook for 1 minute. Add the beef to the pan and toss well, then serve immediately.

 Chilli Beef and Red Pepper Stir-Fry

Slice 300 g (10 oz) frying steak. Heat 1 tablespoon sesame oil in a large wok or heavy-based frying pan and stir-fry the steak with 1 deseeded and finely chopped red chilli and 1 red pepper, cored, deseeded and cut into matchsticks, for 3 minutes. Add 2 tablespoons oyster sauce and cook for a further 1 minute. Serve on a bed of cooked plain rice and scatter with 1 tablespoon chopped chives.

 Quick Crispy Chilli Beef with Broccoli

Thinly slice 300 g (10 oz) thin-cut sirloin steaks and toss with 3 tablespoons seasoned cornflour. Heat 4 tablespoons sesame oil and 2 tablespoons vegetable oil in a large wok or heavy-based frying pan and stir-fry the beef over a high heat for 3–4 minutes until crisp. Remove from the pan with a slotted spoon. Add 1 large head sliced broccoli florets, 1 large carrot, cut into thick batons, 2 sliced garlic cloves, 2 teaspoons peeled and chopped fresh root ginger and ½ teaspoon dried chilli flakes and stir-fry for 3–4 minutes until softened. Add 4 tablespoons light soy sauce mixed with 2 tablespoons sugar and 2 tablespoons sweet chilli sauce, toss well and cook for 1 minute. Return the beef to the pan with 1 bunch of roughly chopped spring onions and heat through. Serve with ready-cooked long-grain rice, heated through according to the packet instructions.

FAM-SNAC-NEU

 # Coconut Soup with Spinach and Butternut Squash

Serves 4

1 tablespoon vegetable oil

1 onion, finely chopped

500 g (1 lb) butternut squash, peeled, deseeded and cut into cubes

1 small red chilli, finely chopped

1 teaspoon ground coriander

400 g (13 oz) can coconut milk

600 ml (1 pint) rich chicken or vegetable stock

300 g (10 oz) spinach leaves

warm naan breads, to serve

- Heat the oil in a large, heavy-based saucepan and cook the onion, butternut squash and chilli over a medium-high heat, stirring frequently, for 8 minutes until softened. Add the coriander and cook, stirring, for a few seconds, then stir in the coconut milk and stock and bring to the boil. Reduce the heat and simmer for 10 minutes.

- Stir in the spinach leaves and cook for 1 minute until just wilted. Ladle the soup into warmed serving bowls and serve with warm naan breads.

 Quick Caribbean-Style Coconut Soup
Heat 1 tablespoon vegetable oil in a large, heavy-based saucepan and cook 1 finely chopped red onion over a medium-high heat, stirring frequently, for 3 minutes. Add 1 teaspoon ground coriander and ½ teaspoon smoked paprika and cook, stirring, for a few seconds. Stir in a 400 g (13 oz) can coconut milk and 600 ml (1 pint) chicken or vegetable stock and bring to the boil. Add a 400 g (13 oz) can drained kidney beans with 300 g (10 oz) spinach leaves and simmer for 5 minutes. Serve with corn bread, if liked.

 Chicken, Butternut and Coconut Noodle Soup Heat 1 tablespoon vegetable oil in a large, heavy-based saucepan and cook 250 g (8 oz) minced chicken over a medium-high heat, stirring to break up the mince, for 5 minutes until browned. Add 1 chopped onion, 500 g (1 lb) butternut squash, peeled, deseeded and cut into cubes, 1 finely chopped small red chilli and a 2.5 cm (1 inch) piece peeled and grated fresh root ginger. Cook, stirring frequently, for 8 minutes. Add 1 teaspoon ground coriander and cook, stirring, for a few seconds, then stir in a 400 g (13 oz) can coconut milk and 600 ml (1 pint) chicken stock. Bring to the boil, then simmer for 10 minutes, adding 300 g (10 oz) ready-cooked Thai rice noodles for the last 3 minutes of cooking time. Serve immediately.

Salami and Sweetcorn Hash with Poached Eggs

Serves 4

500 g (1 lb) ready-prepared
  potato wedges
2 tablespoons olive oil
1 red onion, roughly chopped
1 teaspoon smoked paprika
175 g (6 oz) chunk salami (from
  the deli counter), cut into
  chunks
100 g (3½ oz) frozen sweetcorn
  kernels
6 tablespoons chopped parsley
4 eggs
salt

- Bring a saucepan of lightly salted water to the boil and cook the potato wedges for 5 minutes, then drain. Meanwhile, heat the oil in a large, heavy-based frying pan and cook the onion over a medium heat, stirring frequently, for 5 minutes until softened.

- Add the smoked paprika and drained potato wedges to the onion and toss well, then cook for a further 5 minutes, stirring and breaking up to crisp and brown a little. Add the salami and sweetcorn and cook, stirring, for 3–4 minutes before adding the parsley. Toss well and then press the mixture down a little. Reduce the heat, cover and cook for 2–3 minutes.

- While the hash is cooking, half-fill a frying pan with boiling water and return to the boil. Break the eggs into the water, 2 at a time, and cook for 2 minutes until just cooked. Remove from the pan with a slotted spoon or fish slice.

- Spoon the hash on to warmed serving plates and top each serving with a poached egg.

---

1 **Salami and Thyme
Rosti with Poached
Eggs** Gently break up 400 g
(13 oz) ready-prepared potato
rosti in a bowl. Add 75 g (3 oz)
sliced salami, 1 grated onion,
25 g (1 oz) melted butter and a
few thyme leaves. Season with
salt and pepper and mix well.
Heat a nonstick frying pan, tip in
the mixture and press down with
a spatula. Cook over a high heat
for 4 minutes on each side until
browned. Meanwhile, poach
4 eggs as above and serve on
top of the rosti.

2 **Salami and Red
Pepper Hash with
Baked Eggs** Parboil 300 g (10 oz)
thinly sliced new potatoes in a
saucepan for 5 minutes, then drain.
Meanwhile, heat 2 tablespoons
olive oil in a large frying pan and
cook 1 chopped onion over a
medium heat, stirring frequently,
for 3 minutes. Add the potato
slices and ½ teaspoon dried chilli
flakes and cook, stirring and
breaking up the potatoes, for 4
minutes until browned. Add 175 g
(6 oz) salami, cut into chunks,
and 100 g (3½ oz) chopped

flame-roasted red peppers
from a jar. Mix well, then press
the mixture down and cook
for a further 3 minutes before
sprinkling over a handful of
snipped chives. Make 4 hollows
in the vegetable mixture and
crack an egg into each. Cook
gently for 4 minutes. Take the
pan to the table and serve.

FAM-SNAC-QAK

20 Mushroom and Thyme Soup with Goats' Cheese Croûtes

Serves 4

3 tablespoons olive oil

1 onion, chopped

500 g (1 lb) chestnut mushrooms, trimmed and roughly chopped

2 tablespoons thyme leaves, plus extra to garnish

600 ml (1 pint) chicken or vegetable stock

2 tablespoons Dijon mustard plus 1 teaspoon

200 ml (7 fl oz) crème fraîche

8 thin slices of small French baguette, toasted

8 thin slices of rinded goats' cheese

salt and pepper

- Heat the oil in a large, heavy-based saucepan and cook the onion over a medium heat, stirring occasionally, for 3 minutes. Add the mushrooms and thyme leaves and cook, stirring occasionally, for 5 minutes until the mushrooms are tender and browned. Pour in the stock, add the 2 tablespoons mustard and bring to the boil. Reduce the heat and simmer for 5 minutes.

- Transfer the soup to a food processor and whizz until almost smooth, then return to the pan, add the crème fraîche and season generously with a little salt and some pepper. Heat through for 1 minute.

- Thinly spread the baguette slices with the remaining teaspoon of mustard and place a goats' cheese slice on top of each. Cook under a preheated high grill for 1–2 minutes until the cheese is just beginning to brown in places.

- Serve the soup ladled into warmed serving bowls with the croûtes on top, garnished with extra thyme leaves.

 Mushroom and Thyme Ciabatta Toasts Heat 3 tablespoons olive oil in a large, heavy-based saucepan and cook 1 chopped onion over a medium heat, stirring occasionally, for 3 minutes. Add 500 g (1 lb) trimmed and roughly chopped button mushrooms and 2 tablespoons thyme leaves and cook, stirring occasionally, for 5 minutes until the mushrooms are tender and browned.

Stir in 2 tablespoons wholegrain mustard and 200 ml (7 fl oz) crème fraîche. Toast 4 large slices of ciabatta bread under a preheated grill until golden, spoon a quarter of the mushroom mixture over each toast and garnish with thyme leaves.

30 Rich Mushroom and Thyme Soup Soak 30 g (1 oz) mixed dried mushrooms in 600 ml (1 pint) hot water for 10 minutes, then drain the mushrooms and use the mushroom soaking liquid in place of the chicken stock in the recipe above. Chop the reconstituted mixed mushrooms and add to the onion with the fresh mushrooms and thyme leaves as above.

30 Crisp-Fried Citrusy Calamari with Chilli Sauce

Serves 4

vegetable oil, for deep-frying
500 g (1 lb) squid rings, defrosted
  if frozen
75 g (3 oz) cornflour
2 eggs
finely grated rind and juice of
  1 lime
2 tablespoons finely chopped
  fresh coriander, plus extra to
  garnish
lime wedges, to serve
8 tablespoons sweet chilli sauce
salt and pepper

- Fill a large, deep heavy-based saucepan a third full with vegetable oil and heat to 180–190°C (350–375°F), or until a cube of bread browns in 30 seconds.

- Drain the squid rings very well. Place the cornflour on a plate and season well with salt and pepper. Toss the calamari in the seasoned cornflour and place on a separate plate.

- Beat the eggs thoroughly in a bowl, then add the lime rind and coriander and beat again. Beat in 2 tablespoons of the seasoned cornflour. Dip the squid rings in the batter to coat, quickly add to the hot oil and deep-fry in 2–3 batches, depending on the size of the pan, for 3–4 minutes until golden and crisp. Remove with a slotted spoon and drain on kitchen paper. Meanwhile, mix the lime juice with the chilli sauce and place in a small serving bowl.

- Serve the calamari hot, scattered with coriander to garnish, with lime wedges and the chilli sauce for dipping.

---

1 Pan-Fried Garlicky and Citrusy Calamari

Melt 15 g (½ oz) butter with 2 tablespoons olive oil in a large, heavy-based frying pan and cook 1 sliced garlic clove with 500 g (1 lb) squid rings, defrosted if frozen, over a very high heat, stirring frequently, for 5 minutes until piping hot and browned in places. Finely grate the rind of 1 lemon, add to the pan along with its juice and toss into the squid. Season generously with pepper and then scatter with 4 tablespoons chopped parsley to serve.

2 Spicy and Citrusy Crisp-Fried Prawns

Mix together 125 g (4 oz) fresh white breadcrumbs, ½ teaspoon dried chilli flakes, 3 teaspoons ground cumin, the finely grated rind of 1 lime and ½ teaspoon each salt and pepper. Spread over a plate. Toss 20 large, raw shelled but tail-on prawns in 2 tablespoons seasoned flour on a plate, then dip into 1 beaten egg and finally into the breadcrumb mixture. Heat 3.5 cm (1½ inches) vegetable oil in a large, deep heavy-based frying pan to 180–190°C (350–375°F), or until a cube of bread browns in 30 seconds. Fry the prawns in batches for 2 minutes until crisp and golden. Remove with a slotted spoon and drain on kitchen paper. Serve with a bowl of mayonnaise mixed with the juice from the lime and a handful of chopped fresh coriander.

# Creamy Ham and Mustard Pasta

Serves 4

375 g (12 oz) dried fusilli
1 tablespoon olive oil
25 g (1 oz) butter
1 onion, thinly sliced
25 g (1 oz) plain flour
300 ml (½ pint) milk
1 tablespoon wholegrain mustard
1 teaspoon Dijon mustard
200 ml (7 fl oz) crème fraîche
250 g (8 oz) smoked ham, cut
  into thin strips
4 tablespoons chopped parsley
pepper
rocket salad, to serve (optional)

- Bring a large saucepan of lightly salted water to the boil and cook the pasta for 10–12 minutes until just tender. Drain, return to the pan and toss with the oil.

- Meanwhile, melt the butter in a large, heavy-based saucepan and cook the onion over a medium heat, stirring occasionally, for 5 minutes until softened. Add the flour and cook, stirring, for a few seconds. Remove from the heat and add the milk, a little at a time, blending well between each addition. Return to the heat, then bring to the boil, stirring constantly, cooking until thickened.

- Stir in the mustards, crème fraîche, ham and parsley and heat for a further 1 minute until the sauce is piping hot but not boiling. Stir in the pasta and season with pepper.

- Serve in warmed serving bowls with a simple rocket salad, if liked.

 Instant Ham and Mustard Pasta

Bring a large saucepan of lightly salted water to the boil, add 500 g (1 lb) fresh linguine and cook for 3 minutes or until just tender. Drain the pasta and return to the hot pan. Stir in 250 g (8 oz) smoked ham, cut into thin strips, 1 tablespoon wholegrain mustard, 1 teaspoon Dijon mustard, 4 tablespoons chopped parsley and 150 ml (¼ pint) double cream, toss well and serve immediately.

 Ham, Mustard and Tomato Bake

Make the recipe above, but instead of serving in warmed bowls, pour the pasta mix into a baking dish, top with 3 large, sliced beef tomatoes and sprinkle with 50 g (2 oz) grated Cheddar cheese. Cook under a preheated medium grill for 7 minutes until the tomatoes are softened and the cheese is bubbling and browned.

Brie, Pepper and Spinach Deep-Set Frittata

Serves 4–6

3 tablespoons olive oil
1 red onion, sliced
200 g (7 oz) baby spinach leaves
8 eggs
100 g (3½ oz) drained Peppadew peppers, roughly chopped
175 g (6 oz) Brie, cut into chunks
salt and pepper
leafy salad, to serve (optional)

- Heat the oil in a 25 cm (10 inch), heavy-based frying pan and cook the onion over a medium heat, stirring occasionally, for 5 minutes until softened. Add the spinach and cook, stirring, for 1 minute until wilted. Remove the pan from the heat.

- Beat the eggs in a bowl and season with a little salt and plenty of pepper, then pour over the spinach and onion in the pan.

- Scatter over the Peppadew peppers and Brie evenly and leave them to settle in the frittata mixture. Return the frittata to a low heat and cook for 3–5 minutes until the base is set.

- Place the pan under a preheated medium grill, making sure that the pan handle is turned away from the heat, and cook for 3–4 minutes until the top is golden and set. Serve cut into wedges, accompanied by a simple leafy salad, if liked.

 Brie, Spicy Pepper and Bacon Omelette

Heat ½ tablespoon olive oil in a large frying pan. Snip 6 good-quality rindless smoked back bacon rashers into small pieces and cook over a medium-high heat, stirring frequently, for 3 minutes until crispy. Beat together 4 eggs, season and pour into the pan. Cook for 1 minute, then add 100 g (3½ oz) drained Peppadew peppers, cut into chunks. Sprinkle over 1 tablespoon chopped chives, then scatter over 100 g (3½ oz) Brie, cut into small pieces. Cook for a further 4–5 minutes until just set. Serve with a crusty baguette and cold French butter.

 Spicy Pepper and Pea Tortilla

Heat 1 tablespoon olive oil in a large frying pan and cook 1 chopped onion and 100 g (3½ oz) drained and roughly chopped Peppadew peppers over a medium heat, stirring occasionally, for 5 minutes. Add 1 crushed garlic clove, a drained 400 g (13 oz) can butter beans and 2 tablespoons frozen peas and cook, stirring, for 3 minutes. Beat 6 eggs in a bowl, season and pour over the vegetable mixture in the pan. Sprinkle over 1 tablespoon chopped parsley and cook over a low heat for 5 minutes. Place the pan under a preheated medium grill, making sure that the pan handle is turned away from the heat, and cook for 3–4 minutes until lightly browned. Leave to cool for 2 minutes before cutting into thick wedges to serve.

Thai Chicken Soup

Serves 4

2 x 400 g (13 oz) cans reduced-fat coconut milk
125 ml (4 fl oz) hot chicken stock
1 tablespoon Thai red curry paste
2 boneless, chicken breasts, about 175 g (6 oz) each, very thinly sliced
200 g (7 oz) mangetout
200 g (7 oz) bean sprouts

- Place the coconut milk, stock and curry paste in a large saucepan and bring to the boil.

- Add the chicken and cook for 2 minutes, then add the mangetout and bean sprouts and cook for a further 5 minutes until the chicken is cooked through.

- Serve ladled into warmed serving bowls.

Thai Green Curry Stir-Fry

Heat 2 tablespoons vegetable oil in a large wok or heavy-based frying pan and cook 1 roughly chopped lemon grass stalk, 1 cm (½ inch) piece of fresh root ginger, peeled and roughly chopped, and 4 thinly sliced boneless, skinless chicken breasts, about 150 g (5 oz) each, over a medium-high heat, stirring frequently, for 5 minutes until browned and cooked through. Add 200 g (7 oz) mangetout, 1 cored, deseeded and roughly chopped red pepper and 200 g (7 oz) bean sprouts and stir-fry over a high heat for 2–3 minutes. Blend 1 tablespoon Thai green curry paste with 6 tablespoons coconut milk, then pour over the stir-fry and cook, tossing, for a further 2 minutes.

Chicken and Mangetout Thai Green Curry

Place 2 x 400 g (13 oz) cans coconut milk in a saucepan with 1 roughly chopped lemon grass stalk and a 2.5 cm (1 inch) piece of fresh root ginger, peeled and chopped, 2 roughly chopped fresh kaffir lime leaves, 1 tablespoon Thai green curry paste, 4 boneless, skinless chicken breasts, about 150 g (5 oz) each, cut into chunks, 100 g (3½ oz) mangetout and 2 cored roughly chopped red peppers. Bring to the boil and then simmer for 15–20 minutes. Blend 2 tablespoons cornflour with 2 tablespoons cold water. Remove the pan from the heat and stir in the cornflour mixture. Return to the heat and bring to the boil, stirring, until thickened. Add 8 tablespoons chopped coriander and serve.

FAM-SNAC-SIO

30 Fried Eggy Bread Sandwich with Mozzarella

Serves 4

4 eggs
8 slices of good-quality seeded bread
2 tablespoons vegetable oil
4 tablespoons olive oil
1 aubergine, trimmed and thinly sliced
150 g (5 oz) mozzarella cheese, drained and thinly sliced into 12 slices
handful of spinach leaves
4 tablespoons red pesto
salt and pepper

• Beat the eggs in a large shallow bowl and season with a little salt and pepper. Dip the bread slices into the beaten egg until coated on both sides. Heat the vegetable oil in a large, heavy-based frying pan and cook the bread in batches over a medium-high heat for 30 seconds–1 minute on each side until golden and set. Remove and stack to keep warm.

• Heat the olive oil in the pan and cook the aubergine slices over a medium-high heat for 5–6 minutes, turning once, until browned and tender. Remove and keep warm.

• To assemble, divide the aubergine slices between 4 of the eggy bread slices, cover each with 3 mozzarella slices then top with a few spinach leaves. Spread the remaining eggy bread slices with the pesto and place, pesto-side down, on each stack. Press down well. Return to the warm pan and cook over a low heat for 2 minutes, turning once, until the spinach has wilted and the mozzarella begins to melt. Cut each sandwich in half diagonally and serve warm.

---

 1 **Brie and Pine Nut Eggy Bread with Salsa** Butter 8 slices of good-quality bread, top the buttered side of 4 bread slices with a thick slice of Brie and sprinkle with 2 tablespoons toasted pine nuts. Cover with the remaining bread slices, butter-side down, and cut in half diagonally. Beat 2 eggs with 2 tablespoons milk in a shallow bowl and season. Melt a knob of butter with 1 teaspoon olive oil in a large frying pan. Dip the sandwiches in the egg mixture and cook for 2 minutes on each side. Serve with fresh salsa.

 2 **Roasted Tomato and Pesto Eggy Bread** Cut 4 tomatoes in half and place, cut-side up, in a baking dish. Top each with a basil leaf, drizzle with olive oil and season with salt and pepper. Place in a preheated oven, 200°C (400°F), Gas Mark 6, for 15 minutes. Meanwhile, mix 3 beaten eggs with 1 tablespoon milk, season and pour into a wide dish. Spread 8 slices of good-quality bread on both sides with green pesto from a 145 g (4¾ oz) tub. Dip the bread slices into the egg mixture until coated on both sides. Heat 1 tablespoon olive oil in a large, heavy-based frying pan and cook the bread in 2 batches over a medium-high heat for 1 minute on each side. Serve the eggy bread topped with the roasted tomatoes.

Sweetcorn Fritters with Chilli and Tomato Salsa

Serves 4

275 g (9 oz) can sweetcorn
65 g (2½ oz) plain flour
1 teaspoon baking powder
1 egg, beaten
½ red pepper, finely chopped
1 small red chilli, deseeded and
   finely chopped
6 tablespoons chopped coriander
2 tablespoons vegetable oil
pepper

For the salsa

1 tablespoon olive oil
2 tomatoes, finely chopped
½ small red chilli, finely chopped
1 tablespoon soft light brown sugar
2 tablespoons chopped coriander

· Drain the sweetcorn and place half the kernels in a food processor and whizz until almost smooth. Transfer to a bowl and stir in the remaining, whole sweetcorn. Sift in the flour and baking powder and mix together. Mix in the egg, red pepper, chilli and coriander and season with plenty of pepper.

· Heat the vegetable oil in a large, heavy-based nonstick frying pan over a medium-high heat and drop in 4 spoonfuls of the mixture. Cook for about 1 minute on each side until browned. Remove with a fish slice, drain on kitchen paper and keep warm. Cook the remaining mixture in the same way (to make 8 fritters in total).

· Meanwhile, mix together all the ingredients for the salsa, season with pepper and place in a serving bowl.

· Serve the fritters warm with the salsa on the side.

 Sweetcorn Pancakes

Make up a 150 g (5 oz) packet pancake batter mix according to the packet instructions and mix in 8 tablespoons drained canned sweetcorn and 3 tablespoons chopped coriander. Season well. Heat a little vegetable oil in a frying pan over a medium-high heat, pour in a quarter of the mixture and cook for 1 minute, then turn and cook for a few seconds on the other side. Cook the remaining mixture in the same way. Fill the pancakes with shop-bought tomato salsa and a few rocket leaves, if liked.

 Crab and Sweetcorn Fritters

Whizz half a drained 275 g (9 oz) can sweetcorn kernels in a food processor until almost smooth. Spoon out the light and dark meat from a fresh dressed crab and stir into the puréed sweetcorn with the remaining, whole sweetcorn and 2 finely chopped spring onions. Sift in 65 g (2½ oz) plain flour and 1 teaspoon baking powder and mix together. Mix in 1 beaten egg, ½ finely chopped red pepper, 1 small deseeded and finely chopped red chilli, 6 tablespoons chopped fresh coriander and plenty of pepper. Heat 2 tablespoons vegetable oil in a large, heavy-based nonstick frying pan over a medium-high heat and drop in 4 spoonfuls of the mixture. Cook for about 1 minute on each side until browned. Remove with a fish slice, drain on kitchen paper and keep warm. Cook the remaining mixture in the same way. Serve on salad leaves with a small bowl of salsa as above.

30 Aubergine and Garlic Dip with Toasted Pitta

Serves 4

2 large aubergines
2 teaspoons ground cumin
1 teaspoon ground coriander
1 garlic clove, roughly chopped
150 ml (¼ pint) olive oil
finely grated rind and juice of
  1 lemon
4 tablespoons chopped fresh
  coriander
salt and pepper
pitta breads, to serve

- Trim the aubergines, then slice lengthways into thick slices. Mix the cumin, ground coriander and garlic into the oil, then lightly brush both sides of each aubergine slice with the flavoured oil, reserving the remaining oil.

- Heat a large, heavy-based frying pan over a medium-high heat and cook a third of the aubergine slices for 3–4 minutes, turning once, until softened and lightly browned. Remove from the pan and cook the remaining batches of slices in the same way.

- Place the warm aubergine slices in a food processor with the lemon rind and juice and the reserved flavoured oil. Whizz until almost smooth but with a little texture. Transfer to a bowl, then mix in the fresh coriander and season with a little salt and pepper.

- Griddle or toast the pitta breads until golden and warm, cut into strips and serve with the dip.

1 Quick Baba Ganoush Dip

In a food processor, whizz together a 175 g (6 oz) jar chargrilled aubergines, 2 tablespoons lemon juice, 2 tablespoons tahini, 1 chopped garlic clove, ½ teaspoon salt and a large pinch of ground cumin to a thick purée. Taste and adjust the seasoning. Add 1 tablespoon natural yogurt and whizz again briefly for a less smoky flavour. Transfer to a serving bowl, drizzle with olive oil and sprinkle with chopped parsley. Serve with a crisp salad.

2 Easy Caponata Dip

Heat 2 tablespoons olive oil in a large, heavy-based frying pan and cook 1 chopped onion, 1 chopped celery stick, 1 red and 1 yellow pepper, cored, deseeded and chopped, and 2 sliced garlic cloves over a medium heat, stirring occasionally, for 15 minutes. Add a 100 g (3½ oz) tub chargrilled aubergines from the deli counter, sliced into chunky pieces, a 400 g (13 oz) can chopped tomatoes, 1 tablespoon small capers, a handful of chopped pitted green olives, 1 tablespoon red wine vinegar and 1 teaspoon caster sugar. Warm through and serve with ciabatta bread.

FAM-SNAC-KAG

1 Eggs Florentine

Serves 4

15 g (½ oz) butter, plus extra for
  buttering the muffins
200 g (7 oz) spinach leaves
4 muffins, split in half
4 eggs
3 tablespoons chopped parsley
200 ml (7 fl oz) jar hollandaise
  sauce
salt and pepper

· Half-fill a small saucepan with water and bring to the boil.
  Meanwhile, melt the butter in a large saucepan, add the
  spinach and cook over a medium heat, stirring, for
  1–2 minutes until wilted. Season with salt and pepper.

· Toast the muffins, cut-side up, under a preheated medium
  grill until lightly browned. Meanwhile, poach the eggs, 2 at a
  time, in the boiling water and cook for 1–2 minutes until the
  whites are firm and the yolks soft.

· Butter the warm muffins, then divide the spinach between
  them and top with an egg. Mix the parsley into the hollandaise
  and spoon over the eggs. Serve with ground black pepper.

 **2 Eggs Florentine
with Leek and
Cheese Sauce** Melt 25 g (1 oz)
butter in a saucepan and cook
2 finely sliced leeks over a medium
heat, stirring, for 3–4 minutes
until soft and beginning to brown.
Stir in 25 g (1 oz) plain flour, then
remove from the heat and add
400 ml (14 fl oz) milk, a little at a
time, blending well between each
addition. Add 1 teaspoon prepared
English mustard and stir well,
then return to the heat and bring
to the boil, stirring constantly,
until thickened. Stir in 2 tablespoons
freshly grated Parmesan cheese.
Cook and prepare the spinach,
eggs and muffins as above, then
assemble with the leek and cheese
sauce instead of the parsley
hollandaise, serving with extra
grated Parmesan, if liked.

 **3 Baked Eggs with
Spinach and
Parmesan Butter** Mix 100 g
(3½ oz) softened butter with
2 tablespoons drained and
chopped sun-dried tomatoes
in oil, 2 tablespoons freshly
grated Parmesan cheese and
2 tablespoons chopped basil.
Melt 15 g (½ oz) of the flavoured
butter in a large saucepan and
cook 400 g (13 oz) spinach
leaves over a medium heat for
2–3 minutes until wilted. Spoon
into the base of 4 large ramekin
dishes, then crack an egg over
the top of each. Add a small
knob of the flavoured butter
to the top of each and place in
the preheated oven, 200 °C
(400 °F), Gas Mark 6, for 12–15
minutes until set. Spread the
remaining flavoured butter over

8 thick slices of French baguette,
place on a baking sheet and
place in the oven for the final
5–6 minutes of the cooking time
until golden. Serve the baked
eggs with the toasts.

Cauliflower Cheese Soup

Serves 4

1 cauliflower, trimmed and cut into florets
600 ml (1 pint) chicken stock
300 ml (½ pint) milk
25 g (1 oz) butter
2 leeks, trimmed, cleaned and finely sliced
2 teaspoons prepared English mustard
1 teaspoon ground nutmeg
100 g (3½ oz) Cheddar cheese, grated
3 tablespoons vegetable oil
2 thick slices of white or brown bread, roughly cut into small cubes
½ teaspoon ground paprika
pepper

- Place the cauliflower florets in a saucepan with the stock and milk and bring to the boil. Reduce the heat and simmer for 10 minutes until the cauliflower is tender.

- Meanwhile, melt the butter in a heavy-based frying pan and cook the leeks over a medium heat, stirring occasionally, for 5 minutes.

- Add the mustard and nutmeg to the cauliflower, then stir in the cheese. Transfer to a food processor and whizz until smooth. Return to the pan, stir in the leeks and season with a little pepper. Heat through gently while cooking the croûtons.

- Heat the oil in a large, heavy-based frying pan over a high heat. Toss the bread cubes with the paprika and cook the croûtons, stirring frequently, for 2–3 minutes until golden and crisp. Remove with a slotted spoon and drain on kitchen paper.

- Ladle the soup into warmed serving bowls and scatter the croûtons over the top.

Speedy Spinach and Cheese Soup

Place 600 ml (1 pint) chicken stock and 300 ml (½ pint) milk in a saucepan, add 250 g (8 oz) frozen chopped spinach, 2 teaspoons prepared English mustard and 1 teaspoon ground nutmeg and bring to the boil. Reduce the heat and simmer for 5 minutes, then stir in a 300 g (10 oz) jar cheese sauce and heat for 2 minutes. Serve in warmed serving bowls with shop-bought croûtons.

Classic Cauliflower Cheese

Place 1 cauliflower, trimmed and cut into florets, in a saucepan of water and bring to the boil. Reduce the heat and simmer for 10 minutes. Meanwhile, melt 50 g (2 oz) butter in a saucepan, add 50 g (2 oz) plain flour and cook over a medium heat, stirring, for a few seconds. Remove from the heat and add 600 ml (1 pint) milk, a little at a time, blending well between each addition. Return to the heat, then bring to the boil, stirring constantly, cooking until thickened. Beat in 100 g (3½ oz) grated Cheddar cheese, 2 teaspoons prepared English mustard and 1 teaspoon ground nutmeg. Drain the cauliflower and place in a baking dish, pour over the cheese sauce and sprinkle the top with 50 g (2 oz) grated Cheddar. Cook under a preheated high grill for 5 minutes until browned.

30 Artichoke, Olive and Taleggio Mini Pizzas

Serves 4

150 g (5 oz) packet pizza base mix

plain flour, for dusting

4 tablespoons sun-dried tomato paste

280 g (9 oz) jar artichoke antipasti, well drained

4 tablespoons pitted kalamata olives

100 g (3½ oz) taleggio cheese, sliced

rocket leaves dressed with olive oil and lemon juice, to serve (optional)

- Make up the pizza base mix according to the packet instructions and divide into 4 pieces. Knead each piece briefly on a lightly floured work surface, then roll each into a 12 cm (5 inch) round and place on a baking sheet.

- Spread each round with 1 tablespoon of the tomato paste, then randomly scatter the drained artichokes and black olives over the top.

- Top with the slices of taleggio, tucked between the vegetables and placed over them. Place in a preheated oven, 220°F (425°F), Gas Mark 7, for 12 minutes until the bases are cooked and the tops lightly browned.

- Serve the pizzas hot, with rocket leaves dressed with olive oil and lemon juice, if liked.

 Sun-Dried Tomato and Artichoke Ciabatta Pizzas Slice 2 olive ciabatta loaves in half horizontally. Spread with 4 tablespoons sun-dried tomato paste, then randomly scatter a drained 250 g (8 oz) jar artichoke antipasti and a handful of drained sun-dried tomatoes in oil over the top. Sprinkle over a 160 g (5½ oz) tub mini mozzarella balls and top with a fresh grating of Parmesan cheese. Cook under a preheated high grill for 4–5 minutes until the cheese is lightly browned and bubbling.

 Pancetta, Goats' Cheese and Artichoke Pizzas Place 2 shop-bought ready-made pizza bases on a baking sheet. Spread with 2 tablespoons green pesto, then arrange a drained 250 g (8 oz) jar artichoke antipasti over the top, sprinkle over 75 g (3 oz) cubed pancetta and top with 125 g (4 oz) sliced goats' cheese. Place in a preheated oven, 220°F (425°F), Gas Mark 7, for 12 minutes. Cut each pizza in half and serve with a crunchy herb salad.

QuickCook

Meaty
Suppers

Recipes listed by cooking time

10

3 Chargrilled Chicken with Salsa and Fruity Couscous

Serves 4

4 boneless, skinless chicken
   breasts, about 150 g (5 oz) each
6 tablespoons balsamic vinegar
175 g (6 oz) couscous
350 ml (12 fl oz) boiled water,
   slightly cooled
3 tablespoons olive oil
1 avocado, stoned, peeled and
   roughly chopped
1 large tomato, roughly chopped
5 tablespoons chopped fresh
   coriander
50 g (2 oz) raisins
4 tablespoons pumpkin seeds
salt

- Place the chicken in a non-metallic container, pour over the vinegar and coat. Cover and leave to marinate for 5 minutes.

- Place the couscous in a bowl, pour over the measurement water and season with a little salt. Cover and leave to absorb the water for 10 minutes.

- Meanwhile, heat 1 tablespoon of the oil in a large frying pan or griddle pan and cook the chicken over a medium heat, turning once, for 10–12 minutes until browned and cooked through.

- While the chicken is cooking, make the salsa by mixing together the avocado, tomato, 1 tablespoon of the remaining olive oil and 1 tablespoon of the coriander in a bowl.

- Stir the remaining tablespoon of olive oil into the couscous, then add the raisins, pumpkin seeds and remaining coriander and toss again. Serve on warmed serving plates topped with the chicken, with the salsa spooned over.

1 Sun-Dried Tomato and Chicken

Couscous Cook a 110 g (3¾ oz) pack tomato and onion couscous according to packet instructions. Heat 3 tablespoons oil from a 185 g (6½ oz) tub sun-dried tomatoes in oil in a large saucepan and heat through 400 g (13 oz) ready-cooked chicken breast chunks for 3 minutes. Add 5 chopped sun-dried tomatoes and 1 diced red pepper and cook over a medium heat, stirring, for 5 minutes. Stir in 2 chopped spring onions, 1 tablespoon each clear honey and balsamic vinegar, 1 teaspoon wholegrain mustard and the couscous.

2 Chargrilled Chicken with

Salsa and Lemon Couscous Cook 4 boneless, skinless chicken breasts, about 150 g (5 oz) each, as above. Meanwhile, place 175 g (6 oz) couscous in a bowl, then pour over 300 ml (½ pint) hot chicken stock, cover and leave to absorb for 10 minutes. While the couscous is standing, for the salsa, mix together 1 stoned, peeled and diced mango, 1 small finely chopped red onion, 1 chopped tomato and 1 tablespoon chopped fresh coriander in a serving bowl. In a separate bowl, mix together the finely grated

rind and juice of 1 lemon, 1 tablespoon each olive oil, balsamic vinegar and chopped mint and a pinch of sugar. Pour over the couscous and mix well. Serve the couscous and salsa with the chicken as above.

Sweet and Sour Pork with Fresh Pineapple Chunks

Serves 4

1 tablespoon vegetable oil

½ pineapple, skinned, cored and cut into bite-sized chunks

1 onion, cut into chunks

1 orange pepper, cored, deseeded and cut into chunks

375 g (12 oz) pork fillet, cut into strips

100 g (3½ oz) mangetout, halved lengthways

6 tablespoons tomato ketchup

2 tablespoons soft light brown sugar

2 tablespoons white wine or malt vinegar

cooked egg noodles, to serve (optional)

- Heat the oil in a large, heavy-based frying pan or wok and stir-fry the pineapple chunks over a very high heat for 3–4 minutes until browned in places. Remove with a slotted spoon. Add the onion and orange pepper and cook over a high heat, stirring frequently, for 5 minutes until softened. Add the pork strips and stir-fry for 5 minutes until browned and cooked through.

- Return the pineapple to the pan with the mangetout and cook, stirring occasionally, for 2 minutes. Mix the tomato ketchup, sugar and vinegar together in a jug and pour over the pork mixture. Toss and cook for a further 1 minute to heat the sauce through.

- Serve immediately, with egg noodles, if liked.

 Speedy Sweet and Sour Pork Stir-Fry

Drain the juice from a 435 g (14 oz) can crushed pineapple and blend 5 tablespoons of juice with 2 tablespoons cornflour, add 4 tablespoons rice vinegar and 2 tablespoons each tomato ketchup, dark soy sauce and soft light brown sugar. Heat 1 tablespoon vegetable oil in a large frying pan over a high heat and stir-fry 200 g (7 oz) pork strips for 2 minutes. Add 1 chopped red pepper, stir-fry for 2 minutes, then add 5 shredded spring onions, the pineapple and the pineapple juice mixture, warm through and serve with noodles.

 Roast Sweet and Sour Pork

Mix together 5 tablespoons hoisin sauce, 2 tablespoons Chinese red cooking wine, 2 tablespoons sunflower oil, 1 tablespoon dark soy sauce, 100 g (3½ oz) chopped spring onions and 3 chopped garlic cloves. Pour over 4 pork shoulder steaks, each 175 g (6 oz) in weight, in an ovenproof dish, then drizzle with 1 tablespoon clear honey. Place in a preheated oven, 180°C (350°F), Gas Mark 4, for 20 minutes. Drizzle over another tablespoon of honey and return to the oven for 5 minutes. Meanwhile, heat 1 tablespoon

sesame oil in a large frying pan or wok and stir-fry ½ pineapple skinned, cored and cut into chunks, over a high heat for 3 minutes. Add a handful of pak choi and stir-fry until wilted. Serve the pork over egg noodles with the pineapple and pak choi on top.

Chicken and Tarragon Burgers

Serves 4

500 g (1 lb) boneless, skinless chicken breasts, roughly chopped
1 tablespoon wholegrain mustard
3 tablespoons chopped tarragon
½ small red chilli, finely chopped (optional)
4 wholemeal buns
pepper

To serve

béarnaise sauce from a jar
rocket leaves tossed in lemon juice

- Place the chicken in a food processor and whizz until smooth. Transfer to a bowl, add the mustard, tarragon and chilli and season well with pepper. Mix together until well blended, then shape into 4 patties.

- Lay the chicken burgers on a grill rack lined with foil and cook under a preheated high grill for 4–5 minutes on each side until browned and cooked through. Split the buns and place, cut-side up, under the grill for the final 1 minute of cooking time.

- Place a hot burger on the top of each warm bun base and top with a spoonful of béarnaise sauce and a handful of lemon juice-dressed rocket. Cover with the warm bun tops and serve immediately.

 Crunchy Chicken Burgers with Tarragon Mayonnaise Place 4 boneless, skinless chicken breasts, about 150 g (5 oz) each, between 2 sheets of lightly oiled clingfilm and bash with a rolling pin until half their original thickness. Beat 1 egg with 1 teaspoon Dijon mustard. Place 100 g (3½ oz) fresh white breadcrumbs in a separate bowl. Dip each chicken breast into the egg mixture and then coat in breadcrumbs. Cook under a preheated grill for 4 minutes on each side until crisp and brown. Meanwhile, stir 1 tablespoon chopped tarragon and 1 teaspoon lemon juice into 4 tablespoons mayonnaise. Serve on the burgers in toasted buns, with salad leaves.

Fried Chicken with Tarragon and Sunblush Tomatoes Split 4 boneless, skinless chicken breasts, about 150 g (5 oz) each, in half along their length without cutting all the way through, to produce 'pockets'. Fill each with 4 sunblush tomatoes and 1 large tarragon sprig and secure with kitchen string or a wooden cocktail stick. Heat 2 tablespoons olive oil in a large, heavy-based frying pan and cook the chicken breasts over a medium-high heat for 5 minutes on each side. Pour in 300 ml (½ pint) chicken stock and bring to the boil. Reduce the heat, cover and simmer for 10 minutes. Meanwhile, beat 1 egg with 2 teaspoons Dijon mustard. Very slowly whisk in 200 ml (7 fl oz) vegetable oil until thick and creamy. Stir in 2 tablespoons chopped tarragon and season. Serve the hot chicken breasts on warmed serving plates with the sauce spooned over.

30 Sausage, Rosemary and Mixed Bean Hotpot

Serves 4

1 tablespoon olive oil
12 good-quality sausages
1 red onion, sliced
2 Romero red peppers, cored, deseeded and cut into chunks
1 tablespoon rosemary leaves
400 g (13 oz) can adzuki beans (or any other canned pulse), drained and rinsed
400 g (13 oz) can butter beans, drained and rinsed
400 g (13 oz) can cherry tomatoes
150 ml (¼ pint) beef stock
warm crusty wholemeal bread, to serve (optional)

- Heat the oil in a large, heavy-based frying pan and cook the sausages over a medium heat, turning frequently, for 10 minutes until browned all over and cooked through. Remove with a slotted spoon. Pour off most of the oil from the pan and discard, leaving about 1 tablespoon. Add the onion and red peppers to the pan and cook, stirring frequently, for 3–4 minutes until softened. Add the rosemary leaves and cook for a further 1 minute.

- Add the drained beans, tomatoes and stock and bring to the boil. Return the sausages to the pan, reduce the heat to a simmer and cook for 10 minutes until the beans and sausages are piping hot.

- Serve ladled into warmed serving bowls, with warm crusty wholemeal bread, if liked.

1 Chilli and Black-Eyed Bean Hotpot

Heat 1 tablespoon olive oil in a large, heavy-based saucepan and cook 2 chopped red onions, 1 deseeded and finely chopped green chilli and 1 teaspoon peeled and finely chopped fresh root ginger over a medium heat, stirring occasionally, for 5 minutes. Add 1 teaspoon harissa paste and 100 g (3½ oz) stoned and chopped apricots and mix well. Stir in 2 x 400 g (13 oz) cans cherry tomatoes and a drained 400 g (13 oz) can black-eyed beans and heat through, stirring occasionally, for 5 minutes. Season and serve with prepared couscous and spoonfuls of Greek yogurt stirred through with chopped fresh coriander.

2 Chorizo, Chicken and Chickpea

Hotpot Heat 1 tablespoon vegetable oil in a large saucepan and cook 3 thinly sliced boneless, skinless chicken breasts, about 150 g (5 oz) each, 1 chopped onion and 1 chopped garlic clove over a medium heat, stirring frequently, for 5 minutes. Skin and thickly slice 200 g (7 oz) chorizo sausage and cook with the chicken, stirring, for 2 minutes. Add 2 x 400 g (13 oz) cans chopped tomatoes, a drained 400 g (13 oz) can chickpeas and 1 teaspoon each ground cumin and smoked paprika. Simmer for 10 minutes, season and add chopped parsley. Serve with wild rice.

Mango and Spinach Salad with Warm Peanut Chicken

Serves 4

2 tablespoons sesame oil

2 boneless, skinless chicken
breasts, about 175 g (6 oz) each,
thinly sliced

150 g (5 oz) spinach and
watercress salad

1 large ripe mango, stoned, peeled
and sliced

4 tablespoons crunchy peanut
butter

5 tablespoons coconut milk

2 tablespoons sweet chilli sauce

4 tablespoons water

- Heat 1 tablespoon of the sesame oil in a large, heavy-based frying pan and cook the sliced chicken over a high heat, stirring frequently, for 5–6 minutes until browned and cooked through.

- Meanwhile, place the spinach and watercress salad with the mango in a large serving bowl, drizzle with the remaining sesame oil and toss to mix.

- Add the remaining ingredients to the chicken in the frying pan and cook, stirring, for 1 minute. Toss into the salad and serve while still warm.

Chicken and Mango Kebabs

Cut 3 boneless, skinless chicken breasts, about 175 g (6 oz) each, into cubes and place in a bowl with 4 tablespoons dark soy sauce, a 1 cm (½ inch) piece of fresh root ginger, peeled and chopped, and ½ teaspoon Chinese 5-spice powder. Toss well to coat, cover and leave to marinate for 5 minutes. Meanwhile, stone, peel and cut 1 mango into large chunks. Toss in a bowl with 1 tablespoon sesame oil and 2 tablespoons chopped fresh coriander. Thread the chicken and mango evenly on to 8 metal skewers. Cook the kebabs under a preheated high grill for 8–10 minutes, turning occasionally, until browned and cooked through.

Chicken Stir-Fry with Mango and

Peanut Sauce Heat 1 tablespoon vegetable oil in a large wok or heavy-based frying pan and cook 4 boneless, skinless chicken breasts, about 150 g (5 oz) each, cut into chunky cubes, over a medium-high heat, stirring frequently, for 8–10 minutes until browned and cooked through. Add 2 large carrots, peeled and cut into thick batons, and stir-fry for 5 minutes until softened. Add 1 bunch of trimmed and chopped spring onions and 200 g (7 oz) sugar snap peas and stir-fry for a further 2 minutes, then add ½ stoned mango, peeled and cut into thin slices. Cook, tossing, for 1 minute. Remove from the heat.

Blend 3 tablespoons crunchy peanut butter with 2 tablespoons dark soy sauce and 150 ml (¼ pint) boiling water until smooth. Pour into the stir-fry, return to the heat and cook for 2 minutes, gently tossing to avoid breaking up the mango.

Fillet of Beef with a Mustard Crust and Oven Chips

Serves 4

25 g (1 oz) butter
500 g (1 lb) whole fillet of beef
3 tablespoons wholegrain mustard
1 tablespoon Dijon mustard
3 tablespoons thyme leaves
2 tablespoons chopped parsley
salad, to serve (optional)

For the chips

4 baking potatoes, scrubbed and
    cut into wedges
2 tablespoons olive oil
½ teaspoon sea salt flakes
½ teaspoon English mustard
    powder
3 tablespoons chopped parsley

- For the chips, spread the potato wedges out in a large roasting tin and drizzle with the oil. Toss well to lightly coat the potatoes in the oil, then scatter over the salt and mustard powder and toss again. Place in a preheated oven, 220 °C (425 °F), Gas Mark 7, for 20 minutes.

- Meanwhile, melt the butter in a large, heavy-based frying pan and cook the beef briefly over a high heat, turning frequently, until browned all over and sealed. Transfer to a work surface. Mix the mustards and herbs together and spread over the beef. Place the beef in the roasting tin with the potatoes if there is room, or in a separate roasting tin, and cook in the oven for 15 minutes until cooked through but still pink in the centre.

- Slice the beef into thick or thin slices and serve with the chips tossed in the chopped parsley, accompanied by a simple salad, if liked.

---

1 **Minute Steaks with Rocket Sauce**
In a food processor, whizz together 50 g (2 oz) rocket leaves, reserving a few leaves for garnish, 4 tablespoons hot horseradish sauce, 1 garlic clove, 1 teaspoon Dijon mustard and 200 ml (7 fl oz) half-fat crème fraîche. Heat 1 tablespoon olive oil in a large frying pan and cook 4 thin-cut sirloin steaks, about 150 g (5 oz) each, over a high heat for 1½ minutes on each side. Leave to rest while gently heating through the sauce. Spoon over the steaks, garnish with the reserved rocket and serve with oven chips.

2 **Pepper and Mustard Steaks with Butternut Chips** Place 350 g (11½ oz) ready-prepared butternut squash wedges in a roasting tin and toss in 2 tablespoons olive oil and ½ teaspoon sea salt flakes. Place in a preheated oven, 220 °C (425 °F), Gas Mark 7, for 15–17 minutes until browned and cooked through. Meanwhile, brush 4 sirloin steaks, about 175 g (6 oz) each, with olive oil, then coat with 3 tablespoons crushed mixed peppercorns mixed with 3 tablespoons Dijon mustard. Cook in a preheated griddle pan over a high heat for 6–8 minutes, turning once. Leave to rest for 5 minutes before serving with the butternut chips, a spoonful of good mayonnaise and a leafy salad.

Chicken and Chorizo Jambalaya with Peppers

Serves 4

175 g (6 oz) long-grain rice
1 tablespoon olive oil
250 g (8 oz) piece of chorizo
   sausage, cut into chunky slices
1 onion, chopped
375 g (12 oz) boneless, skinless
   chicken breasts, cut into chunks
1 red pepper, cored, deseeded
   and cut into chunks
1 green pepper, cut into chunks
1 yellow pepper, cut into chunks
2 celery sticks, chopped
2 tablespoons cold water
1 tablespoon cornflour
600 ml (1 pint) chicken stock
400 g (13 oz) can chopped tomatoes
salt and pepper
4 tablespoons chopped parsley

- Bring a saucepan of lightly salted water to the boil and cook the rice for 15 minutes until tender, then drain.

- Meanwhile, heat the oil in a large, heavy-based frying pan and cook the chorizo, onion and chicken over a medium heat, stirring occasionally, for 10 minutes until browned and cooked through. Add the peppers and celery and cook, stirring occasionally, for a further 5 minutes.

- Blend the measurement water with the cornflour, then stir into the stock, add to the pan with the tomatoes and bring to the boil. Reduce the heat and simmer for 5 minutes before adding the cooked rice. Season generously with pepper.

- Serve garnished with the parsley, accompanied by crusty bread and salad, if liked.

---

1 Creole-Style Jambalaya

Heat 1 tablespoon olive oil in a large saucepan and cook 1 chopped onion over a medium heat, stirring occasionally, for 5 minutes. Add 200 g (7 oz) sliced chorizo sausage, 4 cooked skinless chicken breast fillets, about 150 g (5 oz) each, chunkily shredded, and 1 teaspoon Creole spice mix. Cook for 1 minute, then add a 350 g (11½ oz) tub fresh tomato sauce, 100 ml (3½ fl oz) chicken stock and a 600 g (1¼ lb) tub ready-cooked egg-fried rice. Stir, heat through, season and serve.

2 Cajun Chicken Jambalaya

Place 4 boneless, skinless chicken breasts, about 150 g (5 oz) each, in a polythene bag with 1 tablespoon Cajun spice mix and toss until evenly coated. Cook under a preheated high grill for 6 minutes on each side until cooked through. Meanwhile, heat through 500 g (1 lb) ready-cooked long-grain rice according to the packet instructions and tip into a large bowl. Add 250 g (8 oz) fresh pineapple cubes, 25 g (1 oz) finely chopped fresh coriander, 3 chopped spring onions and 1 deseeded and finely chopped red chilli. Mix well and season. Slice the chicken breasts and serve on the warm rice with a spoonful each of fresh salsa and natural yogurt.

30 One-Pan Chicken with Honeyed Roots and Stuffing

Serves 4

NB. do some gravy?

4 boneless, skin-on chicken breasts, about 175 g (6 oz) each

2 large baking potatoes, peeled and cut into chunks

6 parsnips, peeled and cut into chunks

6 carrots, peeled and cut into chunks

4 tablespoons olive oil

75 g (3 oz) packet stuffing mix (flavour of your choice)

2 leeks, trimmed, cleaned and cut into chunks

3 tablespoons clear honey

2 tablespoons chopped flat leaf parsley

salt and pepper

- Arrange the chicken breasts in a large roasting tin with the potato, parsnip and carrot chunks. Drizzle with the oil and toss well to coat the chicken and vegetables in the oil. Season with salt and pepper and place in a preheated oven, 220°C (425°F), Gas Mark 7, for 20 minutes.

- Meanwhile, make up the stuffing according to the packet instructions and shape into 4 balls.

- Add the stuffing balls to the roasting tin with the leeks and return to the oven for 5–6 minutes until the leeks have just softened.

- Remove the stuffing balls from the roasting tin along with the chicken pieces. Add the honey and parsley to the vegetables in the tin and gently toss to coat. Serve the chicken and stuffing with the roasted vegetables.

---

 1 Quick Honeyed Chicken and Vegetables with Stuffing

Make up 100 g (3½ oz) of stuffing mix according to the packet instructions and shape into 4 balls. Cook under a preheated high grill, turning frequently, for 3–4 minutes until browned. Meanwhile, heat 2 tablespoons olive oil in a large frying pan and cook 750 g (1½ lb) frozen Mediterranean vegetables over a high heat, stirring frequently, for 5 minutes. Add 4 ready-cooked skinless chicken breast fillets, about 150 g (5 oz) each, roughly torn, and heat through for 2 minutes. Add 3 tablespoons clear honey and 2 tablespoons chopped parsley and gently mix together. Serve the chicken and vegetables with the stuffing on the side.

2 Ham-Wrapped Sausages with Vegetables and Stuffing

Wrap 8 chipolata sausages with 1 slice of Parma ham each, arrange in a large baking dish and bake in a preheated oven, 200°C (400°F), Gas Mark 6, for 5 minutes. Add 750 g (1½ lb) frozen mixed grilled vegetables to the dish, drizzle with olive oil and bake for 8 minutes. Meanwhile, make up 100 g (3½ oz) of stuffing mix according to packet instructions and form into balls. Add to the dish and bake for 6 minutes. Drizzle the sausages and vegetables with balsamic vinegar and serve.

Mediterranean Vegetable Pan-Fry with Lamb

Serves 4

2 tablespoons olive oil
250 g (8 oz) lamb neck fillet
1 Spanish onion, cut into wedges
2 large courgettes, trimmed and
  cut into chunks
2 teaspoons coriander seeds,
  lightly crushed
½ teaspoon ground cumin
½ teaspoon ground paprika
1 red pepper, cut into chunks
1 garlic clove, sliced
400 g (13 oz) can cherry tomatoes
handful of chopped fresh
  coriander leaves
pepper
warm wholemeal bread, to serve

- Heat the oil in a large, heavy-based frying pan or wok, and cut the lamb into thin slices. Cook the lamb with the onion over a high heat, stirring, for 2–3 minutes until the lamb is browned and the onion slightly softened. Add the courgettes and cook, stirring, for 2 minutes until beginning to soften.

- Add the spices and toss well, then add the red pepper and garlic, reduce the heat and cook over a medium heat for 4–5 minutes until all the vegetables are beginning to soften.

- Add the tomatoes, season generously with pepper and bring to the boil. Reduce the heat, cover and simmer, stirring occasionally, for 5 minutes until the vegetables are tender yet still retaining their shape.

- Stir in the chopped coriander before serving with warm wholemeal bread to mop up the juices.

 Vegetable and Lamb Kebabs

Cut 250 g (8 oz) lamb neck fillet into small chunks, sprinkle with 1 teaspoon each ground cumin and paprika and season with salt and pepper. Thread on to metal skewers with 2 large courgettes, trimmed and cut into chunks, and a 225 g (7½ oz) punnet cherry tomatoes. Lightly brush with olive oil and cook under a preheated high grill for 8 minutes, turning once, until browned and cooked through. Serve with warm pitta breads and shop-bought tsatziki.

 Mediterranean Vegetable and Lamb Braise Heat 2 tablespoons olive oil in a large, heavy-based frying pan or wok and cook 250 g (8 oz) thinly sliced lamb neck fillet and 1 large Spanish onion over a high heat, stirring, for 2–3 minutes until the lamb is browned and the onion slightly softened. Add 2 large courgettes, trimmed and cut into chunks, and cook, stirring, for 2 minutes. Add 2 teaspoons lightly crushed coriander seeds and ½ teaspoon each cumin and paprika and toss well, then add 1 red, 1 orange and 1 green pepper, cored, deseeded and cut into chunks, and 1 sliced garlic clove. Reduce the heat and cook over a medium heat for 4–5 minutes until all the vegetables are beginning to soften. Add a 225 g (7½ oz) punnet cherry tomatoes with 150 ml (¼ pint) rich lamb stock and bring to the boil. Reduce the heat, cover and simmer, stirring occasionally, for 15 minutes.

Teriyaki Beef Sandwiches with Bean Sprout Salad

Serves 4

375 g (12 oz) sirloin steak

2 tablespoons dark soy sauce

1 tablespoon vegetable oil

1 teaspoon Chinese 5-spice powder

2.5 cm (1 inch) piece of fresh root ginger, peeled and grated

1 large ciabatta loaf, cut into 4 chunky pieces

For the salad

100 g (3½ oz) bean sprouts

1 red pepper, cored, deseeded and thinly sliced

4 tablespoons chopped fresh coriander

1 tablespoon sesame oil

6 tablespoons sweet chilli sauce

- Using a very sharp knife, slice the steak into thin shavings, slicing from the top down to the base in sideways slices. Mix together the soy sauce, oil, 5-spice powder and ginger in a bowl. Add the steak and toss well to coat. Cover and leave to marinate for 5 minutes.

- Arrange the bread pieces on a baking sheet and place in a preheated oven, 200°C (400°F), Gas Mark 6, for 10 minutes to heat through.

- Meanwhile, place all the ingredients for the salad in a separate bowl and toss well to mix. Heat a large griddle pan or frying pan, lift the beef from the marinade and cook in batches in a single layer over a high heat for 1 minute on each side.

- Fill the warm ciabatta with the beef and spoon the bean sprout salad on top.

 Quick Steak and Horseradish Cream Sandwiches Season 4 rump steaks, about 150 g (5 oz) each, with salt and pepper and cook in a preheated griddle pan over a high heat for 3 minutes on each side. Remove and leave to rest. Mix together 100 g (3½ oz) crème fraîche, 4 tablespoons horseradish sauce and the juice of 1 lemon. Season to taste. Slice the steaks into 1 cm (½ inch) slices. Fill 8 split crusty rolls with the steak, add a spoonful of the horseradish mixture to each and caramelized onions from a jar. Garnish with watercress.

 New York Deli Beef Sandwiches Thinly slice 300 g (10 oz) cooked lean beef. For the slaw, toss together ½ small chopped red cabbage, ½ finely sliced red onion, the juice of ½ lemon, 1 tablespoon olive oil, a handful of chopped parsley and salt and pepper. For the dressing, whisk together 4 tablespoons each crème fraîche and tomato ketchup. Butter 8 slices of sourdough bread, turn over and spread each unbuttered side with a heaped tablespoon of the dressing. Top each of 4 bread slices with a slice of Gruyère cheese, divide the slaw and beef slices between them and add a scattering of chopped parsley. Cover with the remaining slices of bread, buttered-side up, and press down firmly. Cook the sandwiches in a preheated griddle pan over a high heat until browned on both sides. Serve with cornichons.

Special Fried Rice

Serves 4

2 tablespoons sesame oil
2 eggs, beaten
8 rindless streaky bacon rashers, snipped into pieces
1 bunch of spring onions, trimmed and roughly chopped
100 g (3½ oz) small cooked peeled prawns
100 g (3½ oz) frozen peas
250 g (8 oz) ready-cooked long-grain rice
salt and pepper

- Heat 1 tablespoon of the oil in a large frying pan, pour in the eggs in a thin layer and cook over a medium heat for 1–2 minutes until golden and set. Remove and cut into shreds.

- Add the remaining oil to the pan and stir-fry the bacon and spring onions over a high heat for 2–3 minutes until the bacon is browned and the onions softened. Add the prawns and peas and stir-fry for a further 1 minute. Add the rice and stir-fry for 2–3 minutes until hot.

- Add the shredded omelette to the rice and heat through for a few seconds. Season with salt and pepper and serve immediately.

 Stir-Fried Beef and Chilli Rice

Bring a saucepan of lightly salted water to the boil and cook 200 g (7 oz) easy-cook long-grain rice for 15 minutes until tender, then drain. Meanwhile, heat 1 tablespoon sesame oil in a large wok or heavy-based frying pan and stir-fry 300 g (10 oz) thinly sliced rump steak over a high heat for 3–4 minutes until browned. Add 1 bunch of chopped spring onions and stir-fry for 2 minutes, then add 100 g (3½ oz) peas, defrosted if frozen, and stir-fry for a further 2 minutes until hot. Stir in 75 g (3 oz) chopped toasted cashew nuts, 6 tablespoons chopped coriander and 5 tablespoons sweet chilli sauce and stir-fry for 1 minute to heat through. Add the rice and cook, tossing, for a further 2 minutes.

 Vegetable Fried Rice

Bring a large saucepan of lightly salted water to the boil and cook 200 g (7 oz) easy-cook long-grain rice for 15 minutes until tender, then drain. Meanwhile, heat 3 tablespoons olive oil in a wok or large, heavy-based frying pan and cook 2 finely chopped celery sticks, 1 trimmed, halved and thinly sliced small courgette and 2 peeled and thinly sliced carrots over a high heat, stirring occasionally, for 10 minutes until softened. Set aside. Heat 1 tablespoon sesame oil in a separate large, heavy-based frying pan, pour in the eggs in a thin layer and cook over a medium heat for 1–2 minutes until golden and set. Remove and cut into shreds. Add the drained rice and shredded omelette to the vegetables and toss until well mixed and piping hot. Serve with light soy sauce, if liked.

3 Bacon, Onion and Egg Pan-Cooked Tart

Serves 4

500 g (1 lb) potatoes, peeled and
  thickly sliced
2 tablespoons olive oil
250 g (8 oz) rindless back bacon,
  roughly chopped
1 large onion, sliced
250 g (8 oz) tub ricotta cheese
2 eggs
4 tablespoons chopped parsley
600 ml (1 pint) chicken stock
salt and pepper
salad, to serve (optional)

- Bring a large saucepan of lightly salted water to the boil and cook the potatoes for 10 minutes.

- Meanwhile, heat the oil in a large, heavy-based frying pan and cook the bacon and onion over a medium heat, stirring frequently, for 5 minutes until the bacon has browned and the onion softened.

- Drain the potatoes well, then add to the frying pan and cook, stirring frequently without worrying if the potatoes break up, for 2 minutes.

- Dot spoonfuls of the ricotta over the potato mixture. Beat the eggs and parsley into the stock in a bowl, season with pepper and pour over the potato mixture. Cook gently for 10 minutes, then cook under a preheated high grill for a further 2–3 minutes until golden and set.

- Serve spooned on to warmed serving plates, with a simple salad, if liked.

 Chorizo, Spinach and Onion Omelette

Tip 400 g (13 oz) spinach leaves into a colander and slowly pour a kettleful of boiling water over until wilted. Cool under cold running water, then squeeze out all the liquid. Heat 3 tablespoons olive oil in a large frying pan and cook 1 finely chopped onion and 100 g (3½ oz) ready-sliced chorizo over a medium heat, stirring, for 5 minutes. Beat 6 large eggs in a bowl, season and stir in the spinach. Pour over the chorizo mixture, cook for 4 minutes, then cook under a high grill for 1 minute to set the top.

 Bacon and Onion Tortilla

Thickly slice a 560 g (1 lb 2 oz) drained can new potatoes. Heat 2 tablespoons olive oil in a large, heavy-based frying pan and cook 250 g (8 oz) roughly chopped rindless back bacon and 1 sliced onion over a medium heat, stirring frequently, for 5 minutes. Add the potatoes and cook, stirring frequently without worrying if the potatoes break up, for 2 minutes. Beat 6 eggs in a bowl, season and stir in 4 tablespoons chopped parsley. Pour over the bacon and potato mixture and cook gently for 10 minutes. Grate 25 g (1 oz) Manchego cheese over the top of the tortilla and cook under a preheated high grill for a further 2–3 minutes until lightly browned and set.

Apricot-Glazed Gammon Steaks with Paprika Potatoes

Serves 4

500 g (1 lb) potatoes, peeled and cut into cubes

4 lean gammon steaks, about 100 g (3½ oz) each

3 tablespoons vegetable oil

1 onion, roughly chopped

400 g (13 oz) can apricots in fruit juice, drained and juice reserved

1 teaspoon ground cinnamon

2 teaspoons ground paprika

3 tablespoons chopped parsley

salt and pepper

- Bring a large saucepan of lightly salted water to the boil and cook the potatoes for 10 minutes. Drain.

- Meanwhile, cook the gammon under a preheated high grill for 5–6 minutes on each side until cooked through.

- While the potatoes and gammon are cooking, heat 1 tablespoon of the oil in a large, heavy-based saucepan and cook the onion over a medium heat, stirring frequently, for 3–4 minutes until softened. Add the apricot juice and cinnamon and cook over a high heat for 3 minutes to reduce the liquid by half. Remove from the heat and add the apricots, then pour all the mixture into a food processor and whizz to a thick, textured sauce. Return to the saucepan and heat through gently while finishing the potatoes.

- Heat the remaining oil in a large, heavy-based frying pan and cook the drained potatoes over a high heat, stirring frequently, for 5 minutes until golden and crisp. Sprinkle over the paprika, season with pepper and toss in the parsley.

- Spoon the sauce over the gammon to serve, accompanied by the paprika potatoes.

 Spiced Apricot-Glazed Gammon

Warm 2 tablespoons apricot jam in a small saucepan, then stir in ½ teaspoon ground cumin and season with pepper. Cook 4 lean gammon steaks, about 100 g (3½ oz) each, under a preheated high grill, brushing frequently with the glaze, for 5–6 minutes on each side until cooked through. Serve with a tub of ready-prepared Moroccan couscous.

 Glazed Gammon with Minted Bulgar Wheat Salad Bring a saucepan of water to the boil, add 150 g (5 oz) bulgar wheat and simmer for 8 minutes. Add 150 g (5 oz) frozen peas and 2 trimmed, washed and thinly sliced leeks and simmer for a further 3 minutes. Meanwhile, for the glaze, simmer the juice of 1 orange, 2 tablespoons clear honey and 2 teaspoons each Worcestershire sauce and Dijon mustard in a small saucepan for 2 minutes. Cook 4 lean gammon steaks, about 100 g (3½ oz) each, under a preheated high grill, brushing frequently with the glaze, for 5–6 minutes on each side until cooked through. Meanwhile, drain the bulgar wheat and vegetables, season and stir in 2 tablespoons mint sauce. Cut each gammon steak in half and serve on a bed of the warm bulgar salad.

30 Coq au Vin-Style Chicken Breasts

Serves 4

2 tablespoons plain flour

4 boneless, skinless chicken
  breasts, about 150 g (5 oz) each

2 tablespoons olive oil

100 g (3¾ oz) smoked pancetta,
  chopped

2 large red onions, cut into wedges

1 garlic clove, sliced

1 tablespoon rosemary leaves

300 g (10 oz) chestnut mushrooms,
  kept whole and stalks trimmed

300 ml (½ pint) chicken stock

300 ml (½ pint) red wine

salt and pepper

To serve (optional)

crusty bread

cooked green beans

- Place the flour on a plate and season well with salt and pepper. Roll the chicken breasts in the seasoned flour to lightly coat.

- Heat 1 tablespoon of the oil in a large, deep heavy-based frying pan and cook the pancetta and onions over a medium-high heat, stirring frequently, for 4–5 minutes until the pancetta is cooked and the onions softened. Add the garlic, rosemary and mushrooms and cook, stirring, for a further 2 minutes. Remove the ingredients with a slotted spoon.

- Add the remaining tablespoon of oil to the pan and cook the chicken over a medium-high heat, turning occasionally, for 10 minutes until well browned. Add the stock and wine and bring to the boil. Return the pancetta, onion and mushroom mixture to the pan, then reduce the heat, cover and cook for 7 minutes until the chicken is cooked through and tender. Remove the lid and cook for a further 3 minutes. Serve with crusty bread and cooked green beans, if liked.

---

10 Coq au Pasta

Bring a large pan of salted water to the boil and cook 200 g (7 oz) dried farfalle for 8–10 minutes or until just tender, then drain. Meanwhile, heat 1 tablespoon olive oil in a large frying pan and cook 4 thinly sliced boneless chicken breasts, about 150 g (5 oz) each, with 100 g (3¾ oz) smoked pancetta, chopped, and 1 thinly sliced red onion over a high heat, stirring, for 6–7 minutes until the chicken is cooked. Stir in 200 ml (7 fl oz) crème fraîche and 1 tablespoon wholegrain mustard, add the drained pasta and toss well.

20 Quick Coq au Vin

Slice 4 boneless, skinless chicken breasts, about 150 g (5 oz) each, into thin strips and toss in 2 tablespoons plain flour seasoned with salt and pepper. Heat 2 tablespoons olive oil in a large frying pan and cook the chicken strips, 110 g (3¾ oz) smoked pancetta, chopped, 2 large chopped red onions, 1 sliced garlic clove, 1 tablespoon thyme leaves and 300 g (10 oz) whole small button mushrooms, stalks trimmed, over a medium-high heat, stirring frequently, for 10 minutes until the chicken is cooked through and the vegetables are tender. Pour in 300 ml (½ pint) each chicken stock and red wine and bring to the boil, then simmer for 5 minutes. Serve with crusty bread.

30 Rustic Lamb and Potato Curry

Serves 4

2 tablespoons vegetable oil

1 large onion, roughly chopped

625 g (1¼ lb) lean lamb, cut into cubes

1 small green chilli, roughly chopped (optional)

4 tablespoons korma curry paste

2 x 400 g (13 oz) cans chopped tomatoes

300 ml (½ pint) lamb or chicken stock

2 unpeeled potatoes, roughly cut into cubes

50 g (2 oz) fresh coriander, roughly chopped

150 ml (¼ pint) natural yogurt

• Heat the oil in a large, heavy-based frying pan and cook the onion and lamb over a high heat, stirring frequently, for 5 minutes until the lamb is browned all over and the onion softened.

• Add the chilli, if using, and cook, stirring, for 1 minute. Stir in the curry paste and cook, stirring, for a further 2 minutes. Add the tomatoes, stock and potatoes and bring to the boil. Reduce the heat, cover and simmer for 10 minutes, then remove the lid and cook for a further 10 minutes until the lamb is cooked through and the potatoes are tender.

• Remove from the heat, then scatter over the coriander and spoon in the yogurt, ready to stir in and serve.

---

10 Simple Chicken Curry with Naan

Heat 1 tablespoon vegetable oil in a large, heavy-based pan and cook 3 thinly sliced boneless, skinless chicken breasts, about 175 g (6 oz) each, over a high heat, stirring, for 3 minutes. Stir in a 400 g (13 oz) jar korma curry sauce and 1 chopped tomato and bring to the boil. Add 200 g (7 oz) baby spinach leaves, then reduce the heat, cover and simmer for 5 minutes or until the chicken is cooked before serving on lightly toasted naan breads.

20 Chicken and Potato Curry

Heat 2 tablespoons vegetable oil in a large, heavy-based frying pan and cook 3 roughly sliced boneless, skinless chicken breasts, about 175 g (6 oz) each, and 8 thinly sliced new potatoes over a high heat, stirring frequently, for 5 minutes. Add 4 tablespoons korma curry paste and cook, stirring, for 1 minute. Stir in a 400 g (13 oz) can chopped tomatoes and a 400 g (13 oz) can coconut milk. Bring to the boil, then reduce the heat and cook over a medium heat, stirring occasionally, for 10 minutes. Serve scattered with chopped fresh coriander.

 # Mushroom and Cheese Burgers with Cucumber Salsa

Serves 4

500 g (1 lb) minced steak
1 teaspoon smoked paprika
4 spring onions, thinly sliced
1 egg yolk
1 teaspoon prepared
  English mustard
1 tablespoon olive oil
4 chestnut mushrooms,
  trimmed and sliced
4 good-quality wholemeal buns
4 slices of Emmental or Gruyère
  cheese

For the salsa

¼ cucumber, roughly chopped
2 tablespoons chopped fresh
  coriander
pepper

- Place the minced steak in a bowl with the paprika, spring onions, egg yolk and mustard and mix together with a fork until thoroughly blended. Shape into 4 patties.

- Cook the burgers under a preheated high grill for 10 minutes, turning once, until well browned and cooked through.

- Meanwhile, heat the oil in a large, heavy-based frying pan and cook the mushrooms over a high heat, stirring frequently, for 5 minutes until browned. Make the salsa by simply tossing the cucumber and coriander together, and season with a little pepper.

- Split each roll and serve a burger in each, topped with a slice of cheese to melt, then the mushrooms and a spoonful of salsa.

 Quick and Healthy Mini Burgers

Mix together 300 g (10 oz) lean minced beef, 50 g (2 oz) wholemeal breadcrumbs, 50 g (2 oz) grated carrot, 1 small grated onion, 1 crushed garlic clove, a handful of chopped parsley and 2 teaspoons Worcestershire sauce. Shape the mixture into 8 small patties and cook under a preheated medium grill for 3 minutes on each side until cooked through. Serve in split, toasted wholemeal mini buns with a spoonful of shop-bought fresh tomato salsa.

 Mushroom and Beef Burgers with Tarragon Butter Mix 125 g (4 oz) very soft butter with 2 tablespoons Dijon mustard, 1 tablespoon roughly chopped tarragon, the juice of ½ lemon and salt and pepper. Lay 4 large mushrooms in a roasting dish, fill the hollows with the tarragon butter and drizzle with olive oil. Cover with foil and place in a preheated oven, 200°C (400°F), Gas Mark 6, for 20–25 minutes, basting occasionally. Meanwhile, mix together 500 g (1 lb) minced steak, 2 chopped spring onions,

1 egg yolk and salt and pepper. Shape into 4 patties and cook under a preheated high grill for 10 minutes, turning once, until well browned and cooked through. Serve each burger in a split wholemeal roll, topped with a slice of Emmental or Gruyère cheese, along with a mushroom drizzled with tarragon butter. Serve with a green salad, if liked.

30 Spicy Cajun Chicken Quinoa with Dried Apricots

Serves 4

600 ml (1 pint) chicken stock
100 g (3½ oz) quinoa
100 g (3½ oz) ready-to-eat dried
  apricots, roughly chopped
3 boneless, skinless chicken
  breasts, about 175 g (6 oz) each,
  thinly sliced
2 teaspoons Cajun spice mix
2 tablespoons olive oil
2 red onions, cut into slim wedges
2 bunches of spring onions,
  roughly chopped
6 tablespoons chopped fresh
  coriander

To serve
Greek yogurt
crusty bread (optional)

- Place the stock in a saucepan and bring to the boil, add the quinoa, then simmer for 10 minutes. Stir in the apricots and cook for a further 5 minutes.

- Meanwhile, toss the chicken with the Cajun spice in a bowl to coat. Heat the oil in a large, heavy-based frying pan and cook the chicken and onion wedges over a medium-high heat, stirring frequently, for 10 minutes until the chicken is well browned and cooked through. Add the spring onions and cook for a further 1 minute.

- Drain the quinoa and apricots, then add to the chicken mixture and toss well to mix. Toss in the chopped coriander and serve with spoonfuls of Greek yogurt, with crusty bread, if liked.

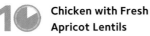 **Chicken with Fresh Apricot Lentils** Heat 1 tablespoon olive oil in a large frying pan and cook 1 finely chopped red onion over a medium heat, stirring frequently, for 5 minutes. Pour in 4 tablespoons red wine vinegar and cook for 30 seconds. Add 250 g (8 oz) ready-cooked Puy lentils, 4 fresh stoned apricots cut into chunks, and 4 tablespoons each chopped fresh coriander and mint. Add 4 cooked chicken breast fillets, about 150 g (5 oz) each, shredded, and heat through for 1 minute. To serve, stir in 50 g (2 oz) rocket.

 Glazed Chicken with Fresh Apricot Quinoa Bring 600 ml (1 pint) chicken stock to the boil in a saucepan, add 100 g (3½ oz) quinoa and simmer for 15 minutes. Meanwhile, mix 3 tablespoons marmalade with 4 teaspoons wholegrain mustard. Slice 4 boneless, skinless chicken breasts, about 150 g (5 oz) each, lay in a roasting tin and brush over half the marmalade glaze. Cook under a preheated high grill for 4–5 minutes, then turn over, brush with the remaining glaze and cook for a further 4–5 minutes. Stone and cut 4 fresh apricots into chunks, then toss with 4 chopped spring onions, 3 tablespoons white wine vinegar and 1 teaspoon ground cumin. Drain the cooked quinoa, stir in the apricot mixture and serve with the chicken, scattered with extra chopped spring onions.

Stir-Fried Duck with Sugar Snaps and Orange Rice

Serves 4

200 g (7 oz) easy-cook
long-grain rice
2 tablespoons sesame oil
1 red onion, cut into slim wedges
4 boneless duck breasts,
skin on, about 150 g (5 oz)
each, thickly sliced
1 bunch of spring onions, cut
into 2.5 cm (1 inch) lengths
175 g (6 oz) sugar snap peas
finely pared rind and juice of
1 orange
2 tablespoons dark soy sauce
1 tablespoon soft light
brown sugar
salt

- Bring a large saucepan of lightly salted water to the boil and cook the rice for 15 minutes until tender. Drain and keep warm.

- Meanwhile, heat the oil in a large wok or heavy-based frying pan over a medium-high heat and stir-fry the red onion for 5 minutes. Add the duck slices and stir-fry for 5 minutes until the duck is almost cooked. Add the spring onions and sugar snap peas and stir-fry over a high heat for 2 minutes.

- Add the drained rice to the pan and toss well. Mix together the orange rind and juice, soy sauce and sugar in a small bowl, then pour over the duck mixture and toss well to distribute the sauce through the dish. Serve immediately in warmed serving bowls.

Chinese Duck Noodles

Heat 2 tablespoons sesame oil in a large wok or heavy-based frying pan over a medium-high heat and stir-fry 4 thickly sliced duck breasts, about 150 g (5 oz) each, for 5 minutes. Add 1 bunch of spring onions, cut into 2.5 cm (1 inch) lengths, and 175 g (6 oz) sugar snap peas and stir-fry over a high heat for 2 minutes. Stir in 300 g (10 oz) ready-cooked Thai rice noodles and 6 tablespoons hoisin sauce and heat through for 2 minutes.

Duck Breasts with Orange

Heat 1 tablespoon sesame oil in a large wok or heavy-based frying pan and cook 4 boneless duck breasts, about 150 g (5 oz each), skin-side down, over a high heat for 5 minutes, then turn over and cook for a further 2 minutes. Transfer to a shallow roasting tin. Add 3 tablespoons each marmalade and orange juice to the wok or frying pan and gently heat for a few seconds, stirring to loosen, then pour over the breasts and place in a preheated oven, 200°C (400°F), Gas Mark 6, while you prepare the rice. Bring a large saucepan of lightly salted water to the boil and cook 200 g (7 oz) easy-cook long-grain rice for 15 minutes until tender, then drain. Heat 2 tablespoons sesame oil in the cleaned wok or frying pan, add 1 bunch of spring onions, chopped, and 175 g (6 oz) sugar snap peas and stir-fry over a high heat for 2 minutes. Add the rice and toss well. Serve with the duck breasts.

Lamb Fillet with Mushroom and Spinach Sauce

Serves 4

2 tablespoons olive oil

2 lamb neck fillet pieces, about 250 g (8 oz) each

For the sauce

15 g (½ oz) butter

250 g (8 oz) chestnut mushrooms, trimmed and halved

100 g (3½ oz) button mushrooms, trimmed

1 small onion, finely chopped

½ teaspoon ground paprika

3 tablespoons brandy

300 ml (½ pint) single cream

250 g (8 oz) baby spinach leaves

• Heat 1 tablespoon of the oil in large, heavy-based frying pan and cook the lamb over a high heat, turning frequently, for 1–2 minutes until browned and sealed all over. Reduce the heat and leave to cook gently while making the sauce, turning once.

• Melt the butter with the remaining tablespoon of oil in a separate large, heavy-based frying pan and cook the mushrooms and onion over a high heat, stirring frequently, for 5 minutes. Add the paprika and cook, stirring, for 1 minute. Add the brandy and cook for a few seconds until the alcohol has evaporated, then remove from the heat and add the cream and spinach.

• Return the pan to the heat, toss and cook for 3–4 minutes over a gentle heat until the spinach has wilted and the sauce is hot.

• Slice the lamb thickly, arrange on warmed serving plates and spoon large spoonfuls of the mushroom and spinach sauce over.

 Quick Lamb Steaks with Creamy Mushrooms Cook 4 lamb loin steaks, about 150 g (5 oz) each, under a preheated high grill for 4–5 minutes on each side. Meanwhile, place 3 tablespoons brandy in a saucepan with a drained 300 g (10 oz) can button mushrooms and heat for around 3 minutes until boiling, then reduce the heat to low, add 300 ml (½ pint) single cream and stir until piping hot but not boiling. Spoon the sauce over the lamb steaks and serve.

 Lamb Meatballs with Mushroom and Spinach Sauce Mix together 500 g (1 lb) finely minced lamb, 2 teaspoons garlic paste and ½ teaspoon paprika and shape into 12 balls. Heat a large, heavy-based frying pan, add the meatballs and cook over a medium-high heat, turning frequently, while making the mushroom and spinach sauce as above. Serve the meatballs drizzled with the sauce.

30 Smoky Chicken and Prawn Paella

Serves 4

2 tablespoons olive oil

2 skinless chicken breasts, about
150 g (5 oz) each, thinly sliced

1 large Spanish onion, thinly sliced

100 g (3½ oz) chorizo, chopped

1 red pepper, chopped

1 green pepper, chopped

2 teaspoons smoked paprika

few saffron threads

250 g (8 oz) Arborio risotto rice

900 ml (1½ pints) hot chicken stock

4 tomatoes, roughly chopped

125 g (4 oz) green beans, trimmed

100 g (3½ oz) frozen peas

200 g (7 oz) large cooked peeled
prawns

salt and pepper

- Heat the oil in a large, heavy-based frying pan and cook the chicken and onion over a medium-high heat, stirring frequently, for 5 minutes until the chicken is well browned and the onion is softened. Add the chorizo and peppers and cook, stirring frequently, for 3 minutes.

- Add the paprika and saffron to the pan and stir well, then add the rice and toss well to coat the grains in the spices. Season with a little salt and pepper. Add the stock and tomatoes and bring to the boil. Reduce the heat, cover and simmer, stirring occasionally and adding more water or stock if necessary, for 10 minutes until the rice is tender.

- Stir in the beans, peas and prawns and cook for a further 5 minutes. Serve immediately.

 1 Simple Smoky Chicken and Prawn Pilaff Heat 2 tablespoons olive oil in a large frying pan and cook 2 very thinly sliced skinless chicken breasts, about 150 g (5 oz) each, 100 g (3½ oz) chopped chorizo sausage and 1 chopped red pepper over a medium-high heat, stirring frequently, for 5–6 minutes until the chicken is cooked through. Add 500 g (1 lb) ready-cooked long-grain rice, 4 chopped fresh tomatoes and 100 g (3½ oz) frozen peas and stir-fry over a high heat for 3 minutes until the rice is hot and the tomatoes are pulpy. Serve with chopped parsley.

 2 Smoky Chicken and Prawn Risotto Place 250 g (8 oz) Arborio risotto or paella rice in a large, heavy-based frying pan with a few saffron threads, ½ teaspoon salt and 1 tablespoon olive oil and cook over a medium heat, stirring, for 1 minute. Add 1.2 litres (2 pints) hot rich chicken stock and bring to the boil. Reduce the heat, cover and simmer for 15 minutes until tender. Meanwhile, in a separate heavy-based frying pan, cook 1 cored, deseeded and chopped red pepper, 1 chopped onion, 100 g (3½ oz) chopped chorizo sausage and 2 sliced boneless, skinless chicken breasts, about 150 g (5 oz) each, over a medium-high heat, stirring frequently, for 10 minutes until the chicken is cooked through. Stir in 1 teaspoon smoked paprika, then toss into the cooked rice with 175 g (6 oz) defrosted frozen peas and 100 g (3½ oz) cooked peeled prawns. Cook for 5 minutes, season well with pepper and serve with freshly grated Parmesan cheese, if liked.

10 Honey-Glazed Pork Chops with Spinach Mash

Serves 4

1 tablespoon clear honey

1 tablespoon wholegrain mustard

4 small pork chops, about 175 g (6 oz) each

100 g (3½ oz) pack instant mashed potato

3 tablespoons crème fraîche

50 g (2 oz) butter

200 g (7 oz) spinach leaves

pepper

- Mix together the honey and mustard, then brush over the chops. Cook under a preheated medium grill for 3–4 minutes on each side or until cooked through.

- Meanwhile, make up the instant mash according to the pack instructions, season with pepper and mix in the crème fraîche. Melt the butter in a large saucepan and cook the spinach over a medium heat, stirring, for 2 minutes until just wilted.

- Stir the spinach into the mash and serve with the pork chops.

 Creamy Pork and Mustard with Instant Mash Heat 2 tablespoons olive oil in a large, heavy-based frying pan and cook 4 thinly sliced pork steaks and 2 red onions, cut into slim wedges, over a medium heat, stirring occasionally, for 7–8 minutes until the pork is browned and cooked through and the onion is tender. Add 150 ml (¼ pint) cider, bring to the boil and continue boiling for 2 minutes until the liquid has reduced by half. Add 200 ml (7 fl oz) crème fraîche and 1 tablespoon wholegrain mustard and season well with salt and pepper. Heat through for 2–3 minutes, then stir in 3 tablespoons chopped parsley. Serve with instant mash, prepared according to the packet instructions.

 Spinach Mash-Topped Pork and Apple Pie Heat 1 tablespoon vegetable oil in a large, heavy based frying pan and cook 500 g (1 lb) minced pork with 1 chopped onion over a medium heat, stirring, for 10 minutes until browned and cooked through. Add a 270 g (9 oz) jar apple sauce and 3 tablespoons chopped sage and cook, stirring occasionally, for a further 5 minutes. Season well, then transfer to a large, shallow gratin dish. Melt 25 g (1 oz) butter in a large saucepan and cook 200 g (7 oz) spinach leaves over a medium heat, stirring, for 2 minutes until wilted. Stir into 2 x 500 g (1 lb) cartons ready-made fresh mashed potato and spoon over the top of the pork. Place under a preheated grill for 5 minutes until piping hot and golden.

Asian-Style Beef Skewers with Satay Sauce

Serves 4

350 g (12 oz) rump or sirloin steak
6 tablespoons dark soy sauce
2 tablespoons sesame oil
2 tablespoons rice vinegar or mirin
1 tablespoon dark brown soft sugar
2.5 cm (1 inch) piece of fresh root
  ginger, peeled and finely grated
1 garlic clove, crushed
crudités, such as carrots, sugar
  snap peas and cucumber

For the sauce

6 tablespoons crunchy peanut
  butter
3 tablespoons dark soy sauce
1 small red chilli, finely chopped
150 ml (¼ pint) boiling water

- Cut the steak into long, thin strips. Mix together the soy sauce, oil, vinegar or mirin, sugar, ginger and garlic in a non-metallic bowl. Add the steak and toss well to coat. Cover and leave to marinate for 15 minutes.

- Meanwhile, heat all the ingredients for the sauce in a pan over a very gentle heat, stirring constantly with a wooden spoon, until smooth and thick. Transfer to a small serving bowl and place on a serving platter with the crudités.

- Thread the beef on to 8 metal skewers, or bamboo skewers presoaked in cold water for 30 minutes, and cook under a preheated high grill for 2 minutes on each side until browned and just cooked.

- Transfer to the serving platter with the sauce and crudités and serve immediately.

 Asian-Style Teriyaki Beef on Lettuce Platters Slice 350 g (11½ oz) trimmed sirloin steak into thin slices and mix with 2 tablespoons bottled teriyaki marinade in a bowl. In a separate bowl, dice ½ cucumber and mix with 2 tablespoons chopped coriander, 1 teaspoon dried chilli flakes and the juice of 1 lime. Heat 1 teaspoon vegetable oil in a large frying pan and cook the steak over a high heat for 1 minute on each side. Pile the cucumber mixture into 8 Little Gem lettuce leaves, top with beef and scatter with chopped spring onions.

 Asian-Style Turkey Satay Kebabs Thread 8 metal skewers alternately with 500 g (1 lb) turkey steaks, cut into cubes, 1 red pepper, cored, deseeded and cut into chunks, and 250 g (8 oz) fresh pineapple chunks, juice reserved. Mix together 200 ml (7 fl oz) coconut cream, a 145 g (4¾ oz) tub satay stir-fry sauce and the pineapple juice, and drizzle about 2 tablespoons over each kebab. Cook under a preheated high grill for 2 minutes on each side. Meanwhile, heat through the remaining satay sauce and stir in 20 g (¾ oz) chopped fresh coriander. Serve the kebabs drizzled with the hot sauce and sprinkled with shredded basil on a bed of cooked egg noodles.

Lamb and Tray-Roasted Vegetables with Chickpeas

Serves 4

1 tablespoon olive oil

8 lamb chops

1 aubergine, trimmed and cut into cubes

1 large red onion, cut into chunks

2 courgettes, trimmed and cut into chunks

1 red pepper, cored, deseeded and cut into chunks

1 yellow pepper, cored, deseeded and cut into chunks

375 g (12 oz) tomatoes, cut into quarters

1 teaspoon ground cumin

1 teaspoon ground coriander

400 g (13 oz) can chickpeas, drained

3 tablespoons pumpkin seeds

- Heat the oil in a large, heavy-based frying pan and cook the lamb chops over a high heat for 1 minute on each side until browned and sealed. Transfer to a large roasting tin with a fish slice, reserving the cooking juices in the pan, and place in a preheated oven, 220°C (425°F), Gas Mark 7, while pan-frying the vegetables.

- Add the aubergine, onion, courgettes and peppers to the frying pan and cook over a high heat, stirring frequently, for 5 minutes. Add the tomatoes and cook, stirring, for 2 minutes.

- Transfer all the vegetables to the roasting tin with the lamb, add the spices and chickpeas and toss to mix. Return to the top shelf of the oven for a further 10 minutes or until the lamb is cooked through.

- Scatter over the pumpkin seeds before serving.

 Moroccan-Style Lamb and Vegetable Stir-Fry Heat 1 tablespoon olive oil in a large, heavy-based frying pan and cook 375 g (12 oz) thinly sliced lamb neck fillet, 1 red and 1 yellow pepper, cored, deseeded and cut into chunks, and 2 courgettes, trimmed and cut into chunks, over a high heat, stirring frequently, for 8 minutes until the lamb is cooked through. Add a squeeze of garlic paste, 1 teaspoon each ground cumin and coriander and a 400 g (13 oz) can chopped tomatoes, stir well and cook for a further 2 minutes.

 Pesto Lamb and Vegetable Bake Prepare the recipe as above, but instead of flavouring the lamb and vegetables with cumin and coriander, make your own green pesto instead. In a food processor, whizz together a handful of basil leaves, 3 tablespoons olive oil, the juice of 1 lemon, 25 g (1 oz) freshly grated Parmesan cheese and 75 g (3 oz) pine nuts until smooth. Toss the pesto into the roasting tin with the lamb, pan-fried vegetables and chickpeas, and bake as above.

FAM-MEAT-ZOO

30 Turkey Meatballs in Rich Tomato and Herb Sauce

Serves 4

500 g (1 lb) minced turkey
50 g (2 oz) fresh white
    breadcrumbs
4 spring onions, thinly sliced
1 tablespoon ground paprika
6 tablespoons chopped parsley
2 tablespoons olive oil
1 onion, finely chopped
2 x 400 g (13 oz) cans chopped
    tomatoes
3 tablespoons sun-dried tomato
    paste
2 tablespoons chopped chives
pepper
cooked rice or noodles, or
    mashed potato, to serve

- Place the minced turkey in a bowl with the breadcrumbs, spring onions, paprika and 3 tablespoons of the parsley and mix together with a fork until thoroughly blended. Shape into 20–24 balls.

- Heat 1 tablespoon of the oil in a large frying pan and cook the meatballs over a medium heat for 20 minutes, turning frequently, until browned all over and cooked through.

- Meanwhile, heat the remaining tablespoon of oil in a separate large, heavy-based frying pan and cook the onion over a medium-high heat, stirring frequently, for 2–3 minutes until just softened. Add the tomatoes and tomato paste and season generously with pepper. Bring to the boil, stirring constantly, then reduce the heat and simmer for 10 minutes until the sauce has reduced a little and thickened.

- Stir the remaining parsley and the chives into the sauce, then stir in the cooked meatballs. Serve with cooked rice or noodles, or mashed potato.

 1 Chickpea and Herb Balls In a food processor, combine 75 g (3 oz) chopped Parmesan cheese, 50 g (2 oz) fresh breadcrumbs, 1 egg, a drained 400 g (13 oz) can chickpeas, 2 garlic cloves, 1 teaspoon dried oregano and a few basil leaves. Shape into 16 balls. Heat 2 tablespoons olive oil in a large frying pan and cook the balls, turning frequently, for 5–6 minutes until browned all over. Meanwhile, warm through a 350 g (11½ oz) tub fresh arrabbiata pasta sauce. Serve the balls over cooked pasta, topped with the sauce.

 2 Moroccan-Style Meatballs Heat 1 tablespoon olive oil in a large, heavy-based frying pan and cook 350 g (11½ oz) ready-prepared beef meatballs over a medium-high heat, turning frequently, for 10 minutes. Remove from the pan, then add 1 large sliced onion and cook, stirring frequently, for 5 minutes. Add 100 g (3½ oz) chopped ready-to-eat dried apricots, 1 teaspoon ground cinnamon, ½ teaspoon ground cumin and a 400 g (13 oz) can chopped tomatoes with garlic. Return the meatballs to the pan and bring to the boil, then simmer for 5 minutes or until cooked through. Serve over prepared plain couscous, sprinkled with chopped fresh coriander and a handful of toasted flaked almonds.

 Pork Escalopes with Prosciutto

Serves 4

4 pork fillets, about 275 g (9 oz)
  each
1 egg, beaten
100 g (3½ oz) fresh white
  breadcrumbs
2 tablespoons chopped parsley
4 tablespoons olive oil
4 thin slices of prosciutto
4 thin slices of Gruyère cheese
pepper

To serve (optional)

green salad
crusty bread

- Place the pork fillets between 2 sheets of lightly greased clingfilm and bash with a rolling pin until half their original thickness and almost doubled in size. Place the beaten egg in a shallow bowl. Mix the breadcrumbs with the parsley on a plate and season with pepper.

- Dip the pork escalopes into the egg to lightly coat and then lightly coat in the herbed breadcrumbs.

- Heat the oil in a large, heavy-based frying pan and cook the pork, in batches if necessary, over a high heat for 1–2 minutes on each side until the breadcrumbs are pale golden. Transfer the pork to a large baking sheet and arrange a slice of prosciutto on top of each and then a slice of Gruyère.

- Place in a preheated oven, 200°C (400°F), Gas Mark 6, for 10 minutes until cooked through and the cheese is melted. Serve with a simple green salad and crusty bread, if liked.

 Sage and Mustard Pork Escalopes

Bash 4 pork fillets, about 275 g (9 oz) each, as in the recipe above. Wrap a rindless back bacon rasher around each, tucking in 2 sage leaves and securing with a wooden cocktail stick. Make a dressing by mixing 2 tablespoons olive oil, 1 tablespoon clear honey, 2 teaspoons each white wine vinegar and wholegrain mustard and 1 teaspoon Worcestershire sauce. Heat 1 tablespoon olive oil in a large frying pan and cook the pork over a high heat for 3 minutes on each side, basting with the dressing throughout.

 Two-Cheese-Crusted Pork Escalopes Bash 4 pork fillets, about 275 g (9 oz) each, as in the recipe above. Season with pepper. Mix together 4 tablespoons fresh white breadcrumbs, 75 g (3 oz) grated mature Cheddar cheese, 30 g (1 oz) melted butter and 1 tablespoon snipped chives. Cook the pork under a preheated high grill for about 3 minutes on one side, then turn over and spread 175 g (6 oz) soft goats' cheese over the uncooked sides. Sprinkle with the breadcrumb mixture and

return to the grill for 3–4 minutes until cooked through. Serve immediately, sprinkled with a few extra chives. Serve with buttered green beans.

30 Sticky Gammon Steaks with Caramelized Onions

Serves 4

1 tablespoon olive oil
4 lean gammon steaks, about
    100 g (3½ oz) each
15 g (½ oz) butter
2 onions, sliced
2 teaspoons thyme leaves
4 tablespoons thick-cut
    marmalade
1 tablespoon wholegrain mustard
300 ml (½ pint) hot chicken stock
instant mashed potato, to serve
    (optional)

- Heat the oil in a large, heavy-based frying pan and cook the gammon steaks over a high heat for 5 minutes, turning once. Remove with a slotted spoon and keep warm.

- Melt the butter in the pan, add the onions and thyme leaves and cook over a low heat, stirring occasionally, for 15 minutes until softened and beginning to caramelize. Stir in the marmalade, mustard and stock and bring to the boil, then gently simmer for 2–3 minutes until beginning to thicken.

- Return the warm steaks to the pan and simmer for a further 3 minutes until the sauce is thick and sticky and the steaks are piping hot. Serve with instant mash, if liked.

10 Sticky Bacon and Onion Pan-Fry

Heat 1 tablespoon olive oil in a large, heavy-based frying pan and cook 12 back bacon rashers, cut into big pieces, and 2 thinly sliced onions over a high heat, stirring frequently, for 4 minutes until the bacon is browned and cooked. Meanwhile, mix together 3 tablespoons each marmalade and orange juice and 1 teaspoon each wholegrain mustard and thyme leaves. Add to the pan and cook, stirring, for 2 minutes until piping hot. Serve as a baked potato filling, cooking the potatoes in a microwave oven, or on thick slices of buttered toast, topped with grated cheese, if liked.

20 Sticky Glazed Gammon Strip

Stir-Fry Cut 4 lean gammon steaks, about 100 g (3½ oz) each, into thin strips. Melt 15 g (½ oz) butter with 1 tablespoon olive oil in a large, heavy-based frying pan and cook the gammon strips with 2 sliced onions, 1 cored, deseeded and sliced orange pepper and 2 teaspoons thyme leaves over a high heat, stirring frequently, for 8–10 minutes until browned and cooked through. Add 100 g (3½ oz) mangetout and cook, stirring frequently, for a further 2 minutes. Mix together 2 tablespoons each marmalade and orange juice and 1 tablespoon dark soy sauce, pour into the pan and toss for 1–2 minutes until the glaze is piping hot and lightly covering all the ingredients. Serve with ready-cooked long-grain rice, heated through according to the packet instructions, if liked.

Creamy Coconut Beef Rendang

Serves 4

250 g (8 oz) Thai jasmine rice
   (optional)
2 tablespoons vegetable oil
1 tablespoon peeled and finely
   chopped fresh root ginger
1 bird's eye chilli, thinly sliced
1 garlic clove, thinly sliced
1 lemon grass stalk, thinly sliced
500 g (1 lb) frying steak, cut into
   strips
½ teaspoon ground cinnamon
pinch of ground turmeric
juice of 1 lime
400 g (13 oz) can reduced-fat
   coconut milk
4 tablespoons chopped fresh
   coriander

- Cook the rice, if using, according to the packet instructions.

- Meanwhile, heat the oil in a large, heavy-based frying pan or wok and cook the ginger, chilli, garlic and lemon grass over a medium heat, stirring frequently, for 1–2 minutes until softened but not coloured. Add the beef, increase the heat to high and stir-fry for 5 minutes until browned and cooked through.

- Stir in the cinnamon and turmeric and cook, stirring, for a few seconds before adding the lime juice and coconut milk. Gently heat, stirring, for 2–3 minutes until the sauce is hot.

- Serve immediately with the cooked jasmine rice, if using, and scatter with the chopped coriander.

---

10 **Speedy Thai-Style Beef and Coconut Skewers** Cut 500 g (1 lb) fillet steak into chunks. Thread on to 8 metal skewers alternately with 2 red peppers, cored, deseeded and cut into chunky pieces. Mix 4 tablespoons Thai red curry paste with 200 ml (7 fl oz) coconut cream and spoon over the skewers. Cook under a preheated high grill for 3–4 minutes on each side or until cooked through. Serve with warm pitta bread.

30 **Coconut and Lemon Grass Beef Skewers** Cut 500 g (1 lb) fillet steak into chunks. Lightly pound the beef chunks and the base of 4 lemon grass stalks with the end of a rolling pin. Pierce each piece of meat top and bottom with a knife, then thread a lemon grass stalk through, thin end first, to form skewers. Mix together 4 tablespoons Thai red or green curry paste and 200 ml (7 fl oz) coconut cream and spoon over the meat. Set aside.

Meanwhile, cook 250 g (8 oz) Thai fragrant rice according to the packet instructions, adding 10 dried kaffir lime leaves at the start of cooking. Cook the skewers under a preheated high grill for 3–4 minutes on each side. Serve with the rice and stir-fried pak choi.

3 Fruity Stuffed Pork Fillet with Rosemary

Serves 4

2 pork fillets, about 250–300 g
(8–10 oz) each

3 tablespoons roughly chopped
rosemary leaves

3 tablespoons olive oil

1 onion, finely chopped

2 fresh peaches, stoned and
roughly chopped

½ teaspoon ground coriander

pinch of ground cumin

pepper

· Lay the pork fillets on a chopping board and make a cut across the meat lengthways through the centre, about 1.5 cm (¾ inch) away from the other side, and open out. Scatter the rosemary leaves over both the inside and then the outside of the meat pieces and season generously with pepper.

· Heat 2 tablespoons of the oil in a large frying pan and cook the onion over a medium heat, stirring, for 4 minutes until softened. Add the peaches and spices and cook for 1 minute.

· Spoon half the peach mixture down the centre of one of the fillets and the remaining mixture down the centre of the other. Gently press the meat back together and tie with kitchen string in several places to hold the stuffing in place.

· Heat the remaining tablespoon of oil in the cleaned frying pan and cook the pork over a gentle heat, turning frequently, for 20 minutes, covering the pan for the final 5–10 minutes of the cooking time, until cooked through and tender.

· Serve the pork hot, sliced into rounds.

1 Fruity Pork Steak Pan-Fry

Mix the juice of 3 oranges with 1 tablespoon chopped rosemary leaves and 2 crushed garlic cloves in a small bowl. Take 4 thin-cut pork loin steaks, about 150 g (5 oz) each, and smear all over with the orange mixture. Heat 1 tablespoon olive oil in a large frying pan and cook the steaks over a high heat for about 3 minutes on each side until cooked through. Serve with prepared plain couscous and lemon wedges, and any juices from the pan.

2 Fruity and Sticky Grilled Pork Steaks

Brush 4 pork steaks, about 150 g (5 oz) each, with a little olive oil, season with salt and pepper and place on a grill pan. Stone and quarter 2 ripe peaches and arrange around the pork. Dot with butter and sprinkle with a pinch of dried chilli flakes and 2 teaspoons muscovado sugar. Cook under a preheated medium grill for 15 minutes, turning halfway through, until the pork steaks are browned and cooked through and the peaches are

soft and sticky. Drizzle any sticky juices in the grill pan over the pork.

30 Poached Chicken with Thai Red Curry Sauce

Serves 4

600 ml (1 pint) chicken stock

1 bunch of spring onions, roughly chopped

2.5 cm (1 inch) piece of fresh root ginger, peeled and roughly chopped

handful of fresh coriander stalks

1 lemon grass stalk, chopped

500 g (1 lb) boneless, skinless chicken breast, cut into cubes

cooked Thai jasmine rice, to serve

For the sauce

1 tablespoon vegetable oil

2 tablespoons Thai red curry paste

200 ml (7 fl oz) coconut cream

4 tablespoons chopped coriander

2 teaspoons Thai fish sauce

- Place the stock, 2 of the spring onions, roughly chopped, the ginger, coriander stalks and lemon grass in a saucepan and bring to the boil. Reduce the heat to a simmer and add the chicken cubes. Poach the chicken for 10 minutes. Remove the chicken with a slotted spoon and set aside (don't worry if some of the flavourings come with the chicken). Strain the stock and reserve 150 ml (¼ pint) in a jug.

- For the sauce, heat the oil in a heavy-based saucepan and cook the remaining spring onions, finely chopped, over a medium-high heat, stirring, for 1 minute. Add the curry paste and cook, stirring, for 1 minute. Add the coconut cream and mix well, then stir in the reserved stock. Add the coriander and fish sauce, return the chicken to the pan and stir well. Heat over a gentle heat for 5 minutes until the sauce has thickened a little and the chicken is piping hot.

- Serve spooned over cooked Thai jasmine rice in warmed serving bowls.

---

10 Quick Thai Red Curry with Coconut Chicken Heat a large wok or frying pan and stir-fry 2 tablespoons Thai red curry paste with a splash of coconut milk from a 400 g (13 oz) can over a medium heat for 1 minute. Pour in the remaining coconut milk and bring up to a simmer. Add 4 sliced skinless chicken breasts, about 150 g (5 oz) each, and 100 g (3½ oz) green beans, and simmer for 5 minutes. Add 100 g (3½ oz) cherry tomatoes and cook for a further 3 minutes. Serve with cooked Thai jasmine rice.

20 Salmon Thai Red Curry Rinse 100 g (3½ oz) green lentils, then place in a saucepan, cover generously with boiling water and simmer for 15 minutes. Meanwhile, heat 1 tablespoon vegetable oil in a large, heavy-based frying pan and cook 1 cored, deseeded and sliced red pepper over a medium-high heat, stirring frequently, for 2 minutes. Add 4 skinless salmon fillets, about 150 g (5 oz) each, cut into cubes, and cook, stirring gently, for 1 minute. Stir in 100 g (3½ oz) Thai red curry paste, a 400 g (13 oz) can coconut milk and 225 g (7½ oz) mangetout, and simmer for 4–5 minutes. Drain the lentils and add to the salmon, then scatter with chopped fresh coriander. Serve with steamed rice.

QuickCook
Fab Fish

Recipes listed by cooking time

30

20

Parmesan-Crusted Haddock with Tomato Avocado Salsa

Serves 4

4 haddock fillets, about 175 g
  (6 oz) each, skin removed
juice of ½ lemon
50 g (2 oz) Parmesan cheese,
  freshly grated
1 teaspoon freshly ground black
  pepper
rocket salad, to serve

For the salsa

1 avocado, stoned, peeled and
  roughly chopped
3 vine-ripened tomatoes, roughly
  chopped
4 tablespoons chopped parsley
2 tablespoons olive oil
pepper

- Place the haddock fillets on a plate and drizzle with the lemon juice. Mix the Parmesan with the pepper on a separate plate. Press the haddock fillets into the Parmesan mixture on one side only to coat.

- Lay the haddock, Parmesan-side up, on a grill rack lined with foil and cook under a preheated high grill for 5–6 minutes until golden and cooked through.

- Meanwhile, mix together all the ingredients for the salsa in a bowl and season with plenty of pepper.

- Serve the hot haddock fillets with the salsa spooned over, with a simple rocket salad and lemon wedges, if liked.

 Tapenade-Crusted Haddock with Tomato Olive Salsa Lay 4 haddock fillets, about 175 g (6 oz) each, skin removed, on a foil-lined grill rack and spread each with 1 tablespoon shop-bought black olive tapenade. Cook under a preheated grill for 5–6 minutes until cooked through. Meanwhile, mix together 1 stoned, peeled and roughly chopped avocado, 3 roughly chopped vine-ripened tomatoes, 4 tablespoons chopped basil, a handful of pitted black olives and 2 tablespoons olive oil in a bowl. Season with pepper and serve with the haddock fillets.

 Parmesan-Crusted Haddock with Vegetable Stew Heat 2 tablespoons olive oil in a heavy-based saucepan and cook 1 teaspoon chopped rosemary leaves and 1 bay leaf over a medium heat for 1 minute. Finely chop 1 onion, 1 large garlic clove, 1 celery stick, 1 carrot and 4 small trimmed courgettes, add to the pan and cook, stirring occasionally, for 7–8 minutes until just tender. Add a drained 400 g (13 oz) can chickpeas and 150 ml (¼ pint) fish stock and simmer for 10 minutes. Meanwhile, prepare and cook

4 haddock fillets, about 175 g (6 oz) each, skin removed, as above. Stir the juice of ½ lemon and 2 tablespoons chopped parsley into the vegetables and serve the haddock on a bed of the stew.

Salmon with Green Vegetables

Serves 4

1 tablespoon olive oil
1 leek, trimmed, cleaned and
   thinly sliced
275 ml (9 fl oz) fish stock
200 ml (7 fl oz) crème fraîche
125 g (4 oz) frozen peas
125 g (4 oz) frozen soya
   (edamame) or broad beans
4 chunky skinless salmon fillets,
   about 150 g (5 oz) each
2 tablespoons snipped chives
instant mashed potato, to serve
pepper

- Heat the oil in a large, heavy-based frying pan and cook the leek over a medium heat, stirring frequently, for 3 minutes until softened. Add the fish stock, bring to the boil and continue boiling for 2 minutes until reduced a little. Add the crème fraîche and stir well to mix. Add the peas, soya (edamame) or broad beans and salmon and return to the boil.

- Reduce the heat, cover and simmer for 10 minutes until the fish is opaque and cooked through and the peas and beans are piping hot.

- Sprinkle over the chives and serve spooned over creamy instant mash with butter and a good grinding of pepper.

 Creamy Salmon and Green Vegetable Pasta Bring a large saucepan of lightly salted water to the boil and cook 500 g (1 lb) fresh tagliatelle for 3–4 minutes or until just tender, then drain. Meanwhile, melt 1 tablespoon butter in a heavy-based frying pan and cook 2 skinless salmon fillets, about 150 g (5 oz) each, cut into small cubes, and 50 g (2 oz) frozen peas over a medium heat, stirring gently, for 3 minutes. Add 16 thin asparagus spears, trimmed and chopped into 3.5 cm (1½ inch) pieces, pour in 75 ml (3 fl oz) fish stock and 275 ml (9 fl oz) single cream and cook gently for a further 5 minutes. Toss the drained pasta into the salmon and cream and serve garnished with torn basil or parsley leaves.

 Salmon and Green Vegetable Quiche In a large, shop-bought ready-made savoury shortcrust pastry case, arrange 1 chopped leek, 50 g (2 oz) frozen broad beans, 50 g (2 oz) frozen peas, 2 tablespoons chopped chives and 2 skinless salmon fillets, about 150 g (5 oz) each, cut into 1.5 cm (¾ inch) cubes. Mix together 2 large eggs, 1 egg yolk, 275 ml (9 fl oz) double cream, a pinch of cayenne pepper and freshly grated nutmeg and pour over the salmon and vegetables. Transfer to a baking sheet and bake in a preheated oven, 180°C (350°F), Gas Mark 4, for 25 minutes until the egg mixture is set and browned.

2 Rich Tomato and Fish Stew

Serves 4

1 tablespoon olive oil

1 onion, thinly sliced

1 garlic clove, chopped

2 tomatoes, roughly chopped

400 g (13 oz) can chopped tomatoes

4 tablespoons sun-dried tomato paste

150 ml (¼ pint) white wine

375 g (12 oz) mixed skinless fish fillets, cut into chunks

175 g (6 oz) raw peeled prawns

5 tablespoons chopped thyme

75 g (3 oz) pitted black olives

pepper

warm crusty bread, to serve

- Heat the oil in a large, heavy-based saucepan and cook the onion and garlic over a medium heat, stirring frequently, for 3–4 minutes until softened. Add the fresh tomatoes and cook, stirring, for 2–3 minutes, then add the canned tomatoes, tomato paste and wine. Bring to the boil and cook over a high heat for 5 minutes until the sauce is thick.

- Stir the fish chunks and prawns into the tomato mixture, then reduce the heat, cover and simmer for 7–8 minutes until the fish is opaque and cooked through and the prawns have turned pink. Stir through the thyme and black olives and season with pepper to taste.

- Serve in warmed serving bowls with warm crusty bread to mop up the juices.

1 Instant Fish Stew

Heat 1 tablespoon olive oil in a heavy-based saucepan and cook 1 finely chopped onion with a squeeze of garlic paste over a medium heat, stirring, for 3 minutes. Add a 400 g (13 oz) can lobster bisque, a 200 g (7 oz) can chopped tomatoes, 175 g (6 oz) mixed skinless fish fillets, cut into chunks, and 175 g (6 oz) cooked peeled prawns and cook over a high heat for 7 minutes until the seafood is cooked through. Serve with crusty bread.

3 Rich Fish Curry

Mix together 1 teaspoon each fennel, cumin and coriander seeds and ground cinnamon, ½ teaspoon each fenugreek seeds and black peppercorns and 1 clove. Spread out on a baking sheet and toast under a preheated high grill for 3–4 minutes. Heat 1 tablespoon olive oil in a large, heavy-based saucepan and cook 1 thinly sliced onion and 1 chopped garlic clove over a medium heat, stirring frequently, for 3–4 minutes until softened. Add 2 roughly chopped tomatoes and cook, stirring, for 2–3 minutes. Add a 400 g (13 oz) can chopped tomatoes, the toasted spices and 150 ml (¼ pint) fish stock. Bring to the boil and then simmer briskly, uncovered, for 10 minutes. Stir in 175 g (6 oz) mixed skinless fish fillets, cut into chunks, and 175 g (6 oz) cooked peeled prawns. Cover and simmer for 7–8 minutes until the seafood is cooked through. Stir through 2 large handfuls of torn fresh coriander and serve.

Crispy Cod Goujons with Lime and Caper Mayonnaise

Serves 4

100 g (3½ oz) plain flour
450 g (1 4½ oz) skinless cod fillet, cut into strips
250 g (8 oz) white breadcrumbs
finely grated rind of 2 limes
1 teaspoon black peppercorns, crushed
2 eggs
150 ml (¼ pint) vegetable oil
salt and pepper

For the mayonnaise

200 ml (7 fl oz) crème fraîche
6 tablespoons mayonnaise
grated rind and juice of 1 lime
2 tablespoons capers, roughly chopped
3 tablespoons chopped parsley
1 tablespoon chopped chives

- Place the flour on a plate and season generously with salt and pepper. Toss the fish strips in the seasoned flour and set aside. Place the breadcrumbs on a separate plate and toss with the lime rind and crushed peppercorns. Beat the eggs thoroughly in a shallow bowl.

- Heat the oil in a large, heavy-based frying pan. Meanwhile, dip each floured goujon in the egg and then in the breadcrumbs, working swiftly until they are all crumbed. Cook in 2 batches over a high heat for 3–4 minutes, turning once until cooked through. Remove with a slotted spoon and drain on kitchen paper.

- While the fish is cooking, for the mayonnaise, mix together the crème fraîche and mayonnaise, then stir in the remaining ingredients and season with pepper. Place in a small serving bowl and serve with the hot goujons.

 Pan-Fried Cod with Lime and Caper Mayonnaise Toss 4 cod loin steaks, about 175 g (6 oz) each, in 50 g (2 oz) plain flour well seasoned with salt and pepper. Heat 4 tablespoons olive oil in a large, heavy-based frying pan and cook over a medium-high heat for 2–3 minutes on each side until golden and cooked through. Meanwhile, make the lime and caper mayonnaise as above. Serve the hot cod steaks with the creamy mayonnaise spooned over.

Lime and Chilli Cod Loin Steaks with Chip Cubes Lightly toss 4 cod loin steaks, about 175 g (6 oz) each, in 50 g (2 oz) plain flour seasoned with salt and pepper. Dip into 2 beaten eggs in a shallow bowl and then 125 g (4 oz) fresh white breadcrumbs mixed with 1 teaspoon chilli flakes. Place on a baking sheet. Cut 3 large baking potatoes into small cubes and toss in 2 tablespoons olive oil. Scatter between the fish on the baking sheet and place in a preheated oven, 200°C (400°F), Gas Mark 6, for 20 minutes until browned and cooked through. Meanwhile, make the lime and caper mayonnaise as above. Serve alongside the fish and chip cubes.

30 Parma Ham and Pesto-Wrapped Monkfish

Serves 4

4 pieces of monkfish tail, about
175 g (6 oz) each

2 tablespoons green pesto

4 slices of Parma ham

2 tablespoons olive oil

500 g (1 lb) fresh tagliatelle

1 bunch of spring onions, trimmed
and thinly sliced

250 g (8 oz) cherry tomatoes,
halved

200 g (7 oz) baby spinach leaves

salt and pepper

· Spread the monkfish tails on one side with the pesto and tightly wrap each with 1 slice of Parma ham. Heat 1 tablespoon of the oil in a large, heavy-based frying pan and cook the monkfish tails over a medium heat, Parma ham-join down, for 3–4 minutes, then turn over and cook on the other side for 3–4 minutes until browned. Transfer to a roasting tin and place in a preheated oven, 200°C (400°F), Gas Mark 6, for 10 minutes.

· Meanwhile, bring a large saucepan of lightly salted water to the boil and cook the tagliatelle for 3–4 minutes or until just tender, then drain. Heat the remaining oil in a large saucepan and cook the spring onions over a medium heat, stirring frequently, for 1–2 minutes until slightly softened. Add the cherry tomatoes and cook, stirring, for 2 minutes, then add the spinach and cook, tossing, for 1 minute until just wilted. Toss in the drained pasta and season generously with pepper.

· Serve the monkfish with the tagliatelle on warmed plates.

 Grilled Salmon with Pesto and Bacon

Place 4 skinless salmon fillets, about 150 g (5 oz) each, on a grill pan and spread each with 1 teaspoon green pesto. Lay 4 rindless streaky bacon rashers next to the salmon and grill the salmon and bacon for 6–8 minutes until the salmon is opaque and cooked through and the bacon is browned and crisp. Serve the salmon fillets on warmed serving plates with a bacon rasher laid across each top.

 Pesto Monkfish and Vegetable Skewers Cut 700 g (1¼ lb) monkfish tail into 2.5 cm (1 inch) pieces. Divide the fish between 4 metal skewers, or bamboo skewers presoaked in cold water for 30 minutes, alternating with 12 cherry tomatoes, 2 courgettes, trimmed and cut into chunks, and 8 bay leaves. Mix 2 teaspoons each of green pesto and olive oil, and drizzle over the skewers. Cook under a preheated high grill or over a barbecue for 15 minutes. Serve with a salad and some crusty bread.

Indian Seafood Biryani

Serves 4

4 eggs
250 g (8 oz) basmati rice
175 g (6 oz) green beans, cut into short lengths
2 tablespoons vegetable oil
2 onions, thinly sliced
3 tablespoons biryani curry paste
175 g (6 oz) large cooked peeled prawns
175 g (6 oz) crab sticks, torn into shreds
6 tablespoons chopped fresh coriander
150 g (5 oz) natural yogurt mixed with 1 teaspoon mint sauce
salt

- Bring a large saucepan of lightly salted water to the boil and cook the eggs and rice in the same pan for 10 minutes. Remove the eggs with a slotted spoon. Add the beans to the pan and cook with the rice for a further 5 minutes until both are tender, then drain. While the beans and rice are cooking, rinse the eggs under cold running water, then shell and roughly chop.

- Meanwhile, heat the oil in a large, heavy-based frying pan and cook the onions over a medium heat, stirring occasionally, for 5 minutes. Add the curry paste and cook, stirring, for 1 minute. Add the prawns and crab sticks and cook, stirring, for 2 minutes until hot.

- Add the drained rice and beans and coriander and cook, stirring, for a further 1 minute. Toss through the chopped eggs, then serve hot with the minted yogurt on the side.

 Speedy Indian Prawn Pilaff

Heat 1 tablespoon vegetable oil in a large frying and cook 1 small grated onion, 2 grated courgettes and 100 g (3½ oz) balti curry paste over a medium heat, stirring frequently, for 3 minutes. Add 200 g (7 oz) frozen peas and cook, stirring frequently, for a further 2 minutes. Add 400 g (13 oz) cooked peeled prawns and cook, stirring, for 2 minutes. Lastly, add 350 g (11½ oz) shop-bought ready-cooked pilau rice and heat through for 2 minutes. Serve sprinkled with 1 teaspoon finely chopped red chilli and a handful of coriander leaves.

 Indian Salmon Biryani with Lentils

Mix 3 tablespoons biryani curry paste with 3 tablespoons natural yogurt. Pour over 4 skinless salmon steaks, about 150 g (3 oz) each), cover and refrigerate. Heat 1 tablespoon olive oil in a heavy-based saucepan and cook 1 chopped red onion over a medium heat, stirring frequently, for 2 minutes. Add 2 crushed garlic cloves, 1 deseeded and finely chopped small red chilli, 2 pinches of ground turmeric, 1 small cinnamon stick, 1 star anise and the crushed seeds from 4 cardamom pods and cook, stirring, for a further 1 minute. Add 100 g (3½ oz) rinsed green lentils and 600 ml (1 pint) vegetable stock and simmer for 5 minutes. Add 150 g (5 oz) basmati rice and simmer for a further 15 minutes. Ten minutes before the rice and lentils are cooked, heat ½ tablespoon olive oil in a frying pan, shake off the marinade from the salmon and cook over a gentle heat for 2–3 minutes on each side, then flake into chunks. Remove the cinnamon stick and star anise from the rice and lentils. Mix in the flaked salmon and 3 tablespoons chopped fresh coriander and serve immediately.

30 Tuna Pasta Gratin with Butternut Squash and Peas

Serves 4

225 g (8 oz) dried penne
2 tablespoons olive oil
1 onion, chopped
1 butternut squash, about 375 g
(12 oz), peeled, deseeded and
roughly chopped into cubes
2 x 200 g (7 oz) cans tuna in oil,
drained and flaked
175 g (6 oz) frozen peas, defrosted
25 g (1 oz) butter
25 g (1 oz) plain flour
300 ml (½ pint) milk
200 ml (7 fl oz) crème fraîche
1 tablespoon Dijon mustard
50 g (2 oz) Cheddar cheese,
grated
salt

- Bring a large saucepan of lightly salted water to the boil and cook the penne for 10–12 minutes until just tender, then drain.

- Meanwhile, heat the oil in a large frying pan or wok and cook the onion and butternut squash over a medium heat, stirring, for 8–10 minutes until softened and golden. Add the drained pasta to the pan and toss together with the tuna and peas.

- Melt the butter in a saucepan, add the flour and cook over a medium heat, stirring, for a few seconds. Remove from the heat and add the milk, a little at a time, stirring well between each addition. Return to the heat, then bring to the boil, stirring constantly, cooking until thickened. Beat in the crème fraîche and mustard. Remove from the heat and stir into the pasta mixture.

- Transfer the mixture to a large gratin dish and sprinkle over the grated Cheddar. Cook under a preheated high grill for 3–4 minutes until the sauce is bubbling and the cheese is browned. Serve with a simple salad.

 Three-Cheese and Tuna Pasta Bring a large saucepan of salted water to the boil and cook 500 g (1 lb) fresh tagliatelle for 3–4 minutes, then drain and add back to the pan. Meanwhile, heat through 1 garlic baguette according to the pack instructions. Add a 350 g (11½ oz) tub fresh three-cheese pasta sauce, 1 tablespoon Dijon mustard, 2 x 200 g (7 oz) cans tuna in oil, drained and flaked, and 175 g (6 oz) defrosted frozen peas to the pasta, and heat through until piping hot. Serve with the garlic bread.

 Tuna, Pasta and Cannellini Bean Salad Drain and reserve the oil from 2 x 200 g (7 oz) cans tuna in oil. Drain and rinse a 400 g (13 oz) can cannellini beans and add to 450 g (14½ oz) cooked chilled pasta shapes with the flaked tuna. Whisk together 3 tablespoons of the reserved tuna oil, 3 tablespoons olive oil, 2 crushed garlic cloves, 1 teaspoon English mustard powder, the finely grated rind of 1 lemon and pepper, then stir through the pasta mixture. Finish with a scattering of thinly sliced red onion and shavings of Parmesan cheese. Serve with warm ciabatta.

FAM–FAB–KYE

 Creamy Scallops with Leeks

Serves 4

50 g (2 oz) butter
16 shelled and cleaned scallops, halved
1 rindless streaky bacon rasher, roughly snipped
3 leeks, trimmed, cleaned and sliced
200 ml (7 fl oz) crème fraîche
finely grated rind of 1 lemon
pepper
quick-cook long-grain rice, to serve

- Melt half the butter in a large, heavy-based frying pan and cook the scallops and bacon over a high heat, stirring frequently, for 2 minutes until just golden and cooked through. Remove with a slotted spoon and keep warm.

- Add the remaining butter to the pan and cook the leeks over a medium heat, stirring occasionally, for 5 minutes until softened and lightly browned in places. Add the crème fraîche and lemon rind and season generously with pepper.

- Return the scallops to the pan and toss into the creamy leeks. Serve immediately with quick-cook rice.

 Creamy Scallop, Leek and Bacon Pasta Bring a large saucepan of lightly salted water to the boil and cook 200 g (7 oz) dried fusilli for 10–12 minutes until just tender. Drain, return to the pan and keep warm. Meanwhile, melt 25 g (1 oz) butter in a large, heavy-based frying pan and cook 8 chopped rindless streaky bacon rashers and 16 shelled and cleaned scallops, sliced in half, over a medium heat, stirring gently, for 2 minutes. Add 4 trimmed, cleaned and sliced leeks and cook, stirring frequently, for a further 5 minutes. Keep warm. Heat 25 g (1 oz) butter in a saucepan, add 25 g (1 oz) plain flour and cook over a medium heat, stirring, for a few seconds. Remove from the heat and add 250 ml (8 fl oz) milk, a little at a time, stirring well between each addition. Return to the heat, then bring to the boil, stirring constantly, cooking until thickened. Remove from the heat and stir in 4 tablespoons freshly grated Parmesan, then 200 ml (7 fl oz) crème fraîche and 3 tablespoons chopped parsley. Add the scallop mixture and sauce to the drained pasta, toss well and serve.

Scallop and Bacon Kebabs with Leeks Cut 10 smoked streaky bacon rashers in half and wrap each around 20 shelled and cleaned small scallops. Thread on to 4 metal skewers. Mix 2 tablespoons olive oil with 1 tablespoon clear honey and brush over the bacon. Melt 25 g (1 oz) butter with 1 tablespoon olive oil in a frying pan and cook 2 finely sliced leeks, stirring, for 6–8 minutes until soft and golden. Add 1 teaspoon each finely grated lemon rind and wholegrain mustard and 200 ml (7 fl oz) crème fraîche and heat for 2 minutes. Keep warm. Heat a griddle pan over a high heat and cook the skewers for 2–3 minutes on each side until brown and cooked through. Serve on a bed of the creamy leeks.

30 Salmon, Leek and Pea Pie with Dill Mash

Serves 4

500 g (1 lb) skinless salmon fillet
25 g (1 oz) butter
25 g (1 oz) plain flour
450 ml (¾ pint) milk
3 large leeks, trimmed, cleaned and sliced
125 g (4 oz) frozen peas, defrosted
2 x 500 g (1 lb) cartons ready-made fresh mashed potato
50 g (2 oz) dill, roughly chopped
25 g (1 oz) Parmesan cheese, freshly grated
salt and pepper

- Place the salmon in a microwave-proof container and pour over 2 tablespoons water. Cover and cook in a microwave oven on high for 3–4 minutes until the fish is opaque and cooked through. Set aside and then flake into large chunks.

- Melt the butter in a saucepan, add the flour and cook over a medium heat, stirring, for a few seconds. Remove from the heat and add the milk, a little at a time, stirring between each addition. Then bring to the boil, stirring, until thickened. Remove from the heat and season with salt and pepper.

- Add the leeks and peas to the sauce, then gently stir in the salmon. Transfer to a large gratin dish. Place the mashed potato in a large bowl and beat with 2 tablespoons water and two-thirds of the dill until soft and smooth. Spoon over the salmon mixture and scatter over the Parmesan. Place in a preheated oven, 200°C (400°F), Gas Mark 6, for 10 minutes, then transfer to a preheated high grill and cook for 5 minutes until the top is browned. Scatter with the remaining dill.

 Quick Salmon, Spinach and Pea Mash Heat a 350 g (11½ oz) tub fresh cheese sauce in a saucepan over a medium heat for 5 minutes. Add 100 g (3½ oz) frozen chopped spinach and 75 g (3 oz) frozen peas and heat, stirring, until the spinach has wilted. Stir in 2 x 212 g (7¼ oz) cans red salmon, drained and flaked, and heat through briefly. Meanwhile, heat 2 x 500 g (1 lb) cartons ready-made fresh mashed potato following the carton instructions until piping hot. Spoon the hot sauce over the mash and serve.

 Oven-Baked Salmon with Leeks and Cheese Place 4 skinless salmon fillets, about 150 g (5 oz) each, in a roasting tin and season well. Melt 25 g (1 oz) butter in a large, heavy-based frying pan and cook 1 trimmed, cleaned and thinly sliced large leek over a high heat, stirring frequently, for 3 minutes until softened. Spoon over the salmon fillets, then top each with 1 tablespoon freshly grated Parmesan cheese. Place in a preheated oven, 200°C (400°F), Gas Mark 6, for 10–12 minutes until the fish is cooked through. Scatter with chopped dill to serve.

Warm Bang Bang Prawn Salad with Thai Noodles

Serves 4

100 g (3½ oz) Thai rice noodles
finely grated rind and juice of
  1 lime
1 tablespoon sesame oil
125 g (4 oz) mangetout
1 bird's eye chilli, thinly sliced
2.5 cm (1 inch) piece of fresh root
  ginger, peeled and roughly
  chopped
250 g (8 oz) large cooked
  peeled prawns
4 tablespoons smooth
  peanut butter
4 tablespoons light soy sauce
150 ml (¼ pint) boiling water
50 g (2 oz) dried pineapple
  pieces, roughly chopped

- Place the noodles in a heatproof bowl, cover with boiling water and leave to soak following the packet instructions until tender. Drain well and toss with the lime rind.

- Meanwhile, heat the oil in a large wok or heavy-based frying pan and stir-fry the mangetout, chilli and ginger over a high heat for 2 minutes. Add the prawns and stir-fry for 2 minutes or until hot. Place the peanut butter, lime juice and soy sauce in a jug, add the measurement water and mix well. Pour into the pan and toss the ingredients together.

- Add the drained noodles and pineapple pieces and gently toss to coat all the ingredients in the sauce. Serve immediately in warmed serving bowls.

 Bang Bang Skewered Prawns

Thread each of 8 small metal skewers with 3 large raw peeled prawns. Cook under a preheated high grill for 3 minutes on each side until they have turned pink. Meanwhile, in a jug, mix 4 tablespoons each smooth peanut butter and light soy sauce with the juice of 1 lime. Serve the sauce in small, individual bowls alongside the skewered prawns and 2 peeled carrots, 2 celery sticks and ½ large cucumber, cut into matchsticks.

 Bang Bang Prawns with Egg-Fried Rice

Bring a saucepan of lightly salted water to the boil and cook 250 g (8 oz) easy-cook long-grain rice for 15 minutes until tender, then drain. Return to the pan, add 75 g (3 oz) cooked peas, 2 trimmed and finely chopped spring onions, 75 g (3 oz) roasted peanuts, 1 beaten egg and 2 tablespoons each sesame oil and light soy sauce and cook over a medium-high heat, stirring, until the egg is cooked. Set aside. Heat 1 tablespoon sesame oil in a large wok or heavy-based frying pan and stir-fry 125 g (4 oz) mangetout, 1 thinly sliced bird's eye chilli and a 2.5 cm (1 inch) piece of fresh root ginger, peeled and roughly chopped, over a medium-high heat for 2 minutes. Add 250 g (8 oz) large cooked peeled prawns and stir-fry for 2 minutes. In a jug, mix 4 tablespoons each smooth peanut butter and light soy sauce with 150 ml (¼ pint) boiling water, then blend in 1 tablespoon cornflour. Add to the pan and heat, stirring, until thickened. Serve over the egg-fried rice.

30 Creamy Haddock Gratin

Serves 4

625 g (1¼ lb) skinless haddock fillet

600 ml (1 pint) milk

1 bay leaf

40 g (1½ oz) butter

40 g (1½ oz) plain flour

50 g (2 oz) Gruyère cheese, grated

½ teaspoon prepared English mustard

salad, to serve

For the topping

100 g (3½ oz) fresh white breadcrumbs

25 g (1 oz) Gruyère cheese, finely grated

finely grated rind of 1 lemon

2 tablespoons chopped parsley

- Place the haddock in a saucepan with the milk and bay leaf, bring to the boil and continue boiling for 3 minutes. Remove the fish with a slotted spoon, reserving the milk, and divide between 4 individual gratin dishes.

- In a separate saucepan, melt the butter, add the flour and cook over a medium heat, stirring, for a few seconds. Remove from the heat and add the reserved milk, a little at a time, stirring well between each addition. Return to the heat, then bring to the boil, stirring constantly, cooking until thickened. Remove from the heat and add the grated Gruyère and mustard.

- Pour the sauce over the fish, dividing it evenly between the dishes. Mix together the ingredients for the topping and scatter over the sauce. Place on the top shelf of a preheated oven, 220°C (425°F), Gas Mark 7, for 10 minutes until the topping is golden and the sauce bubbling. Serve with a simple salad.

---

1 Haddock Ceviche
Chop 250 g (8 oz) very fresh skinless haddock as finely as you can and place in a wide, shallow non-metallic dish. Sprinkle with 1 teaspoon sea salt, ½ teaspoon dried oregano and 75 ml (3 fl oz) lime juice. Cover and leave to marinate for 8 minutes. Drain the fish, discarding the white milky liquid. Add 3 chopped spring onions, 1 chopped green chilli and 4 tablespoons chopped fresh coriander. Serve spoonfuls of the ceviche on pieces of toasted baguette.

2 Cheat's Crunchy Haddock Gratin

Place 625 g (1¼ lb) skinless haddock fillet in a saucepan with 100 ml (3½ fl oz) milk and a bay leaf. Bring to the boil and continue boiling for 3 minutes. Meanwhile, gently heat through a 350 g (11½ oz) tub fresh cheese sauce in a separate saucepan. Drain the fish well, discarding the milk, and transfer to a large gratin dish, then pour over the sauce. In a food processor, whizz together a packet of cheese-flavoured tortilla chips with 2 tablespoons chopped parsley until crumbs form. Sprinkle all over the sauce. Place on the top shelf of a preheated oven, 220°C (425°F), Gas Mark 7, for 10 minutes until the topping is browned and the sauce bubbling.

1 Rich Tomato, Wine and Fish Stew

Serves 4

2 x 400 g (13 oz) jars tomato
  sauce with peppers and onion
150 ml (¼ pint) white wine
1 tablespoon olive oil
375 g (12 oz) skinless white fish
  fillets, torn or cut into chunks
175 g (6 oz) raw peeled prawns
25 g (1 oz) parsley, chopped
pepper

- Place the tomato sauce, wine and oil in a large, heavy-based saucepan and bring to the boil.

- Reduce the heat, add the fish and prawns and simmer for 7 minutes until the fish is opaque and cooked through and the prawns have turned pink.

- Add the parsley and season with pepper, then serve in warmed serving bowls with warm crusty bread.

2 Rich Salmon and Bacon Stew

Heat 1 tablespoon olive oil in a large, heavy-based saucepan and cook 6 roughly chopped rindless smoked streaky bacon rashers over a high heat, stirring frequently, for about 3 minutes until browned. Add 2 x 400 g (13 oz) jars tomato sauce with peppers and onion with 150 ml (¼ pint) white wine and bring to the boil. Reduce the heat to a simmer and add 4 skinless salmon steaks, about 150 g (5 oz) each, cut into chunky cubes, along with 250 g (8 oz) cherry tomatoes and 3 tablespoons chopped rosemary leaves. Bring to the boil and then simmer briskly, uncovered, for 15 minutes until the salmon is cooked through and the cherry tomatoes are tender. Serve with warm crusty bread to mop up the juices.

3 Mediterranean Fish Stew with Chunky Vegetables

Heat 1 tablespoon olive oil in a large, deep frying pan and cook 2 trimmed and chunkily chopped courgettes, 1 cored and deseeded Romero red pepper and 1 yellow pepper, each cut into chunks, and 1 finely chopped red onion over a medium heat, stirring occasionally, for 8–10 minutes until softened. Add 500 g (1 lb) mixed skinless white fish fillets, cut into chunks, 175 g (6 oz) cooked peeled prawns, 2 x 400 g (13 oz) jars tomato pasta sauce and 300 ml (½ pint) white wine and cook, stirring very gently occasionally, for 10 minutes or until the fish is cooked through. Stir in 100 g (3½ oz) pitted black olives and serve in warmed serving bowls topped with 75 g (3 oz) shop-bought ready-made croûtons.

Lemony Prawns and Broccoli Stir-Fry

Serves 4

175 g (6 oz) easy-cook long-grain rice

250 g (8 oz) tenderstem broccoli, trimmed and cut into 7 cm (3 inch) lengths

3 tablespoons vegetable oil

1 large red onion, sliced

1 bunch of spring onions, trimmed and roughly chopped

250 g (8 oz) cooked peeled prawns

finely grated rind and juice of 1 lemon

3 tablespoons light soy sauce

salt

- Bring a saucepan of lightly salted water to the boil and cook the rice for 10 minutes. Add the broccoli to the pan and cook with the rice for a further 5 minutes until both are tender. Drain well and keep warm.

- Meanwhile, heat the oil in a large, heavy-based frying pan or wok and cook the onion over a medium-high heat, stirring frequently, for 5 minutes until softened. Add the spring onions and prawns and stir-fry for 4 minutes.

- Add the lemon rind and juice and soy sauce to the pan and stir well, then add the drained rice and broccoli and stir-fry for 1 minute until all the ingredients are piping hot and well mixed. Serve immediately.

Prawn and Broccoli Noodles Bring a saucepan of water to the boil and cook 200 g (7 oz) medium egg noodles for 3 minutes, then drain. Trim each stem of 250 g (8 oz) tenderstem broccoli and cut lengthways into 3. Heat 3 tablespoons vegetable oil in a large, heavy-based frying pan or wok and stir-fry the broccoli with 1 roughly chopped bunch of spring onions, 250 g (8 oz) cooked peeled prawns and 2 small heads shredded pak choi over a medium-high heat for 4 minutes. Add the finely grated rind and juice of 1 lemon and 3 tablespoons light soy sauce and stir well. Add the drained noodles and toss until piping hot.

Duck, Prawn and Broccoli Gingered Rice Bring a saucepan of lightly salted water to the boil and cook 175 g (6 oz) easy-cook long-grain rice for 10 minutes. Add the broccoli to the pan and cook with the rice for a further 5 minutes until both are tender. Drain well and keep warm. Meanwhile, heat 2 tablespoons sunflower oil in a large, heavy-based frying pan or wok, add 1 thinly sliced boneless duck breast, about 175 g (6 oz), and stir-fry over a medium-high heat for 5 minutes. Remove with a slotted spoon. Add 1 large sliced red onion and cook, stirring frequently, for 5 minutes until softened. Add 1 bunch of trimmed and roughly chopped spring onions and 250 g (8 oz) cooked peeled prawns and stir-fry for 4 minutes. Add a 3.5 cm (1½ inch) piece of fresh root ginger, peeled and grated, and 3 tablespoons light soy sauce and stir well. Return the duck to the pan with the rice and broccoli and stir-fry for 1 minute.

30 Jamaican Spiced Salmon with Corn and Okra

Serves 4

4 skinless salmon fillets, about
   175 g (6 oz) each
1 tablespoon Jamaican jerk
   seasoning
4 corn on the cobs, halved
3 tablespoons olive oil
1 red onion, sliced
250 g (8 oz) okra, trimmed
50 g (2 oz) butter
½ teaspoon paprika
½ teaspoon ground nutmeg
salt

- Rub each of the salmon fillets with the Jamaican jerk seasoning and set aside.

- Bring a large saucepan of lightly salted water to the boil and cook the corn on the cob pieces for 15 minutes until tender.

- Heat 2 tablespoons of the oil in a large, heavy-based saucepan and cook the onion over a medium heat, stirring frequently, for 2 minutes. Add the okra and cook, stirring frequently, for 4 minutes until beginning to soften. Drain the cobs well, add to the pan with the butter and spices and toss for a further 2–3 minutes until lightly browned in places.

- Meanwhile, heat the remaining tablespoon of oil in a large, heavy-based frying pan and cook the salmon fillets, spice-side down, over a medium heat for 3–4 minutes, then turn over and cook for a further 2 minutes until cooked through. Serve hot with the corn and okra mixture.

 Warm Jamaican Spiced Salmon Salad

Rub 4 skinless salmon fillets, about 175 g (6 oz) each, with 1 tablespoon Jamaican jerk seasoning. Heat 1 tablespoon olive oil in a large, heavy-based frying pan and cook the salmon fillets, spice-side down, over a medium heat for 3–4 minutes, then turn over and cook for a further 2 minutes until cooked through. Divide 150 g (5 oz) mixed salad leaves between 4 serving plates. Drain a 200 g (7 oz) can sweetcorn kernels and thinly slice ½ red onion. Divide between the plates. Flake the salmon over the salad and serve with lime wedges for squeezing over.

 Short-Cut Jamaican Spiced Salmon

Follow the recipe above, but instead of boiling the corn on the cob pieces for 15 minutes, place in a microwave-proof bowl with 4 tablespoons water and cover. Cook in a microwave oven on high for 6 minutes.

1 Prawn Spaghetti with Tomato, Garlic and Basil Sauce

Serves 4

500 g (1 lb) fresh spaghetti
2 tablespoons olive oil
2 garlic cloves, sliced
2 x 400 g (13 oz) cans chopped
   tomatoes
3 tablespoons sun-dried tomato
   paste
250 g (8 oz) large cooked peeled
   prawns
25 g (1 oz) basil, roughly chopped
salt and pepper
freshly grated Parmesan cheese,
   to serve (optional)

- Bring a large saucepan of lightly salted water to the boil and cook the spaghetti for 3 minutes or until just tender, then drain.

- Meanwhile, heat the oil in a large, heavy-based frying pan and cook the garlic over a medium heat for a few seconds to flavour the oil, then add the tomatoes and tomato paste and cook, stirring occasionally, for 5 minutes until thickened.

- Add the prawns and basil, stir through and heat through for 1–2 minutes until the prawns are piping hot. Season generously with pepper, then add the drained pasta and toss with the sauce to mix.

- Serve in warmed serving bowls, sprinkled with freshly grated Parmesan cheese, if liked.

---

 2 **Spicy Tomato, Garlic, Seafood and Bacon Pasta** Bring a large saucepan of lightly salted water to the boil and cook 500 g (1 lb) fresh spaghetti for 3 minutes or until just tender. Drain and return to the pan. Heat 2 tablespoons olive oil in a large, heavy-based frying pan and cook 1 finely chopped red chilli and 2 sliced garlic cloves over a medium heat, stirring, for 2 minutes. Add 8 roughly chopped rindless streaky bacon rashers and cook, stirring frequently, for a further 2 minutes. Add 200 g (7 oz) well-drained prepared small scallops and 200 g (7 oz) large cooked peeled prawns and cook over a high heat, stirring frequently, for 3–4 minutes. Add 2 x 400 g (13 oz) cans chopped tomatoes and 3 tablespoons sun-dried tomato paste and cook, stirring occasionally, for 5 minutes until thickened. Stir in 25 g (1 oz) chopped parsley, then add to the drained pasta and toss to coat.

 3 **Prawn, Tomato and Garlic Bake** Cook 500 g (1 lb) fresh penne per packet instructions, then drain. Meanwhile, heat 2 tablespoons olive oil in a large pan and cook 2 sliced garlic cloves over a medium heat, stirring, for 2 minutes. Add 6 tablespoons sun-dried tomato paste and 2 x 400 g (13 oz) cans chopped tomatoes. Bring to the boil, then simmer, uncovered, for 10 minutes until the sauce has reduced by a quarter. Add 4 tablespoons chopped basil, then toss the pasta into the sauce. Transfer to a gratin dish and scatter over 100 g (3½ oz) grated Gruyère cheese. Cook under a high grill for 5 minutes until golden.

10 Pan-Fried Cod and Chips with Lemon Mayo and Dill

Serves 4

4 tablespoons vegetable oil

4 baking potatoes, peeled and cut into cubes

1 tablespoon olive oil

4 pieces of cod loin, about 150 g (5 oz) each

juice and finely grated rind of 1 lemon

4 tablespoons snipped dill

6 tablespoons mayonnaise

salt and pepper

- Heat the oil in a large, heavy-based frying pan and cook the potatoes over a medium-high heat, turning frequently, for 7–10 minutes until golden and crisp.

- Meanwhile, heat the olive oil in a separate large frying pan and cook the cod loins over a high heat for 3–5 minutes, turning once, until golden and cooked through. Squeeze the lemon juice over the fish and season with salt and pepper.

- Mix the lemon rind and half the dill into the mayonnaise and serve with the fish and chips. Scatter the remaining dill over the fish to serve.

2 Pan-Fried Cod and Prosciutto with Sweet Potatoes

Heat 3 tablespoons vegetable oil in a large, heavy-based frying pan and cook 4 peeled and cubed sweet potatoes over a medium-high heat, turning frequently, for 8–10 minutes until browned and soft. Keep warm. Meanwhile, wrap each of 4 pieces of cod loin, about 150 g (5 oz) each, with a slice of prosciutto. Heat 1 tablespoon vegetable oil in a separate frying pan and cook the fish over a medium-high heat, turning occasionally, for 8–10 minutes until golden and cooked through. Mix 6 tablespoons mayonnaise with the finely grated rind of ½ lemon and 3 tablespoons chopped parsley. Serve with the potatoes and pan-fried cod.

3 Roasted Cod Wrapped in Bacon with Oven Chips

Cut 4 peeled baking potatoes into chip-sized pieces and toss with 2 tablespoons vegetable oil. Spread over a baking sheet in a single layer, then place in a preheated oven, 220°C (425°F), Gas Mark 7, for 20 minutes until golden and soft. Meanwhile, wrap each of 4 pieces of cod loin, about 150 g (5 oz) each, with a rindless smoked back bacon rasher, adding 2–3 basil leaves between the fish and the bacon. Place in a roasting tin and season generously. Place in the oven with the potatoes for 15 minutes until the fish is opaque and cooked through. Serve with the chips, scattered with chopped parsley, if liked.

30 Garlic and Tomato Seafood Spaghetti

Serves 4

225 g (7½ oz) dried spaghetti
3 tablespoons olive oil
2 garlic cloves, sliced
3 shallots, cut into slim wedges
1 celery stick, thinly sliced
4 tomatoes, roughly chopped
400 g (13 oz) can chopped
    tomatoes
150 ml (¼ pint) white wine
1 tablespoon chopped thyme
3 tablespoons chopped parsley
250 g (8 oz) large cooked peeled
    prawns
240 g (7¾ oz) packet frozen raw
    mixed seafood, defrosted
salt
warm crusty bread, to serve
    (optional)

· Bring a large saucepan of lightly salted water to the boil and cook the spaghetti for 8–10 minutes until just tender. Drain and keep warm.

· Meanwhile, heat the oil in a large, heavy-based frying pan and cook the garlic, shallots and celery over a medium heat, stirring occasionally, for 3–4 minutes until slightly softened. Add the fresh tomatoes, increase the heat and cook, stirring occasionally, for 2–3 minutes. Stir in the canned tomatoes and wine.

· Bring the tomato mixture to the boil, then reduce the heat slightly to a brisk simmer and cook for 8–10 minutes until the sauce has reduced by a third. Add the herbs, prawns and mixed seafood and cook for 3–4 minutes until the seafood is opaque and all is piping hot. Add the drained spaghetti and toss well to coat in the sauce.

· Serve in warmed serving bowls with warm crusty bread to mop up the juices, if liked.

---

10 Speedy Seafood Pot
Heat 25 g (1 oz) butter with a drop of wok oil in a wok with a lid and stir-fry 250 g (8 oz) large cooked peeled prawns and a 240 g (7¾ oz) packet frozen cooked mixed seafood over a high heat until the seafood is opaque. Stir in 125 ml (4 fl oz) white wine, cover, shake the pan and leave to cook for 3 minutes. Add 4 tablespoons sherry, re-cover and cook for a further 3 minutes, shaking the pan occasionally. Serve in the pan, sprinkled with chopped parsley, with warm crusty bread.

20 Seafood Paella
Melt 25 g (1 oz) butter in a large, nonstick frying pan and cook 1 finely chopped onion, a pinch of saffron threads, 2 cored, deseeded and diced red peppers and 2 chopped tomatoes over a medium heat, stirring occasionally, for 3–4 minutes until softened. Add 250 g (9 oz) quick-cook long-grain rice, 250 g (8 oz) large raw peeled prawns, a 240 g (7¾ oz) packet defrosted frozen raw mixed seafood and 2 tablespoons white wine and simmer for 3 minutes. Add 150 ml (¼ pint) vegetable stock and simmer for a further 5–6 minutes until the prawns have turned pink, the seafood is opaque and the rice is tender. Stir in 3 tablespoons chopped parsley. Serve immediately, garnished with parsley sprigs and lemon wedges.

30 Cheesy Tuna and Sweetcorn Fishcakes

Serves 4

300 g (10 oz) ready-made fresh mashed potato

½ teaspoon ground black pepper

50 g (2 oz) Cheddar cheese, finely grated

200 g (7 oz) can tuna in oil, drained and flaked

100 g (3½ oz) frozen sweetcorn kernels, defrosted

3 tablespoons chopped parsley

175 g (6 oz) fresh wholemeal breadcrumbs

1 egg

vegetable oil, for shallow-frying

To serve

shop-bought hollandaise sauce

rocket salad dressed with lemon juice

- Place the mashed potato in a bowl with the pepper and Cheddar and beat well until smooth. Stir in the tuna, sweetcorn and parsley and mix well. Shape into 8 patties.

- Place the breadcrumbs on a plate. Beat the egg in a shallow bowl. Dip each of the patties in the egg and lightly brush, then lightly coat in the breadcrumbs.

- Heat 6–8 tablespoons vegetable oil in a large, heavy-based frying pan and cook the fishcakes in 2 batches over a medium-high heat for 4–5 minutes, turning once, until golden and crisp. Remove with a fish slice, drain on kitchen paper and keep the first batch warm while cooking the remainder.

- Serve the fishcakes hot with spoonfuls of hollandaise sauce and a simple rocket salad dressed with lemon juice.

---

10 Tuna and Sweetcorn Melts

Mix together a 200 g (7 oz) can tuna in oil, drained and flaked, 100 g (3½ oz) defrosted frozen sweetcorn kernels and 2 tablespoons mayonnaise. Cut a ciabatta loaf in half lengthways and then each piece in half again. Spread each piece of bread with the tuna mixture and grate 25 g (1 oz) Cheddar cheese over the top. Cook under a preheated medium-high grill for 2 minutes or until golden. Serve immediately with a green salad.

20 Creamy Tuna and Sweetcorn Fusilli

Bring a large saucepan of lightly salted water to the boil and cook 225 g (7½ oz) dried fusilli for 10–12 minutes until just tender, then drain. Meanwhile, melt 25 g (1 oz) butter in a saucepan, add 25 g (1 oz) plain flour and cook over a medium heat, stirring, for a few seconds. Remove from the heat and add 300 ml (½ pint) milk, a little at a time, stirring well between each addition. Add 50 g (2 oz) grated Cheddar cheese. Return to the heat, then bring to the boil, stirring constantly, cooking until thickened. Add a 200 g (7 oz) can tuna in oil, drained and flaked, 100 g (3½ oz) defrosted frozen sweetcorn kernels and 3 tablespoons chopped parsley to the sauce. Drain the pasta, toss with the sauce and serve immediately in warmed bowls.

Cajun Spiced Salmon Frittata with Peppers

Serves 4

1 tablespoon olive oil

1 red pepper, cored, deseeded and cut into chunks

1 green pepper, cored, deseeded and cut into chunks

1 small onion, sliced

1 small red chilli, finely chopped

6 tablespoons chopped fresh coriander, plus extra to garnish

250 g (8 oz) skinless salmon fillets

2.5 cm (1 inch) piece of fresh root ginger, peeled and roughly chopped

2 teaspoons Cajun spice mix

6 eggs

pepper

salad, to serve

- Heat the oil in a 23 cm (9 inch) nonstick frying pan and cook the peppers, onion and chilli over a medium heat, stirring occasionally, for 3–4 minutes until beginning to soften. Stir in the coriander, then make a well in the centre of the pan, add the salmon fillets and cook for 3–4 minutes, turning once, until almost cooked through.

- Flake the fillets into chunky pieces in the pan, then add the ginger and spice mix to the pan and gently toss all the ingredients together. Beat the eggs in a jug and season with a little pepper. Pour over the vegetables and salmon and gently cook for 3–4 minutes until the base of the frittata is set.

- Place the pan under a preheated medium grill, making sure that the pan handle is turned away from the heat, and cook for 4–5 minutes until the top is golden and set. Cut into wedges and serve with a simple salad.

Simple Cajun Salmon

Mix a squeeze of ginger paste with 2 teaspoons Cajun spice mix and rub into the flesh of 250 g (8 oz) skinless salmon fillets. Heat 3 tablespoons olive oil in a large frying pan and cook the salmon over a medium heat for 9 minutes, turning halfway through cooking until the fish is cooked through. Serve with bread and salad.

Cajun Salmon Fishcakes

Heat 1 tablespoon olive oil in a large, heavy-based frying pan and cook 1 cored, deseeded and diced red pepper, 1 small diced onion and 250 g (8 oz) skinless salmon fillets for 9 minutes, turning halfway through cooking until cooked through. Flake the salmon into small pieces in the pan, then place in a large bowl with the pepper and onion and 225 g (7½ oz) instant mashed potato, made up according to the pack instructions. Mix together with 2 teaspoons Cajun spice mix, a 2.5 cm (1 inch) piece of fresh root ginger, peeled and grated, 6 tablespoons chopped fresh coriander and 1 beaten egg. Shape into 8 large fishcakes. Heat 3 tablespoons olive oil in the frying pan and cook over a medium-high heat for about 5 minutes on each side until browned. Serve with oven chips and salad.

30 Prawn and Parmesan Tagliatelle with Wilted Spinach

Serves 4

250 g (8 oz) dried tagliatelle
2 tablespoons olive oil
1 red onion, thinly sliced
1 bunch of spring onions, trimmed
  and sliced
1 garlic clove, sliced
300 g (10 oz) raw peeled prawns
200 g (7 oz) baby spinach leaves
2 x 200 g (7 oz) tubs mascarpone
  cheese
50 g (2 oz) Parmesan cheese,
  freshly grated
salt and pepper
warm crusty wholemeal bread, to
  serve (optional)

- Bring a large saucepan of lightly salted water to the boil and cook the tagliatelle for 8–10 minutes until just tender, then drain.

- Meanwhile, heat the oil in a large, heavy-based frying pan and cook the onion over a medium heat, stirring occasionally, for 5 minutes until softened. Add the spring onions and garlic and cook, stirring frequently, for 2 minutes. Add the prawns and cook over a high heat, stirring, for 2 minutes, then add the spinach leaves and cook, stirring constantly, for 1–2 minutes until the spinach has wilted and the prawns have turned pink.

- Add the mascarpone and stir through until melted and hot. Season with plenty of pepper, then add the Parmesan and drained pasta. Heat through, tossing, for 1–2 minutes until piping hot.

- Serve in warmed serving bowls with warm crusty wholemeal bread, if liked.

 Prawn Noodle Stir-Fry

Cook 200 g (7 oz) egg noodles according to packet instructions, then drain. Meanwhile, heat 2 tablespoons groundnut oil in a large wok and stir-fry 1 chopped red chilli and 2 sliced garlic cloves over a high heat for 1 minute. Add 500 g (1 lb) cooked peeled prawns and stir-fry for 3 minutes until hot. Add 300 g (10 oz) ready-prepared mixed stir-fry vegetables and 2 tablespoons each light soy sauce and sweet chilli sauce. Add the drained noodles and toss until piping hot.

 Prawns with Chilli, Spinach and Cheese

Place 500 g (1 lb) raw peeled prawns in a non-metallic bowl and add the juice of 2 limes and a splash of Tabasco sauce. Cover and leave to marinate for 10 minutes. Meanwhile, heat 2 tablespoons olive oil in a large, heavy-based frying pan and cook 2 thinly sliced red onions and 2 crushed garlic cloves over a medium heat, stirring frequently, for about 3 minutes. Add 1 teaspoon dried chilli flakes and cook, stirring, for a further 2 minutes. Transfer to a large gratin dish and scatter with a well-drained 400 g (13 oz) can cooked spinach. Drain the prawns and add to the dish. Season well, then pour over 200 ml (7 fl oz) double cream and sprinkle 125 g (4 oz) each ready-grated mozzarella cheese and freshly grated Parmesan cheese on top. Cook under a preheated high grill for about 10 minutes until browned. Serve scattered with fresh coriander leaves and a loaf of fresh French bread.

30 Roasted Smoked Haddock with Mash and Poached Eggs

Serves 4

750 g (1½ lb) potatoes, peeled and roughly chopped

5 tablespoons milk

50 g (2 oz) butter

4 tablespoons chopped flat leaf parsley

4 pieces of smoked haddock, about 250 g (8 oz) each

4–5 drops lemon juice or malt vinegar

4 eggs

200 ml (7 fl oz) jar hollandaise sauce

salt and pepper

- Bring a large saucepan of lightly salted water to the boil and cook the potatoes for 20 minutes until tender. Drain, return to the pan and mash with the milk and butter. Season generously with pepper and stir through the parsley.

- Meanwhile, place the fish in a roasting tin and place in a preheated oven, 200°C (400°F), Gas Mark 6, for 15 minutes until opaque and cooked through.

- Half-fill a saucepan with water and bring to the boil. Once at a rolling boil, add the lemon juice or vinegar. Stir the water, then break an egg into the water as it's moving and cook the egg for 1–2 minutes until the white is set and the yolk cooked to your liking. Remove with a slotted spoon and keep warm while cooking the remaining eggs in the same way.

- Divide the mash between 4 warmed serving plates, top each serving with a fish fillet and then place a poached egg on the top. Spoon over the hollandaise, or serve in a separate dish, and finish with a grinding of black pepper.

 Smoked Salmon and Egg Muffins

Cook 4 poached eggs as above. Meanwhile, split and lightly toast 4 English muffins. Place on serving plates and divide 250 g (8 oz) smoked salmon slices between the toasted muffins. Top each serving with a poached egg, spoon over a 200 ml (7 fl oz) jar hollandaise sauce and sprinkle with chopped parsley.

 Smoked Haddock Kedgeree with Eggs

Cook 150 g (5 oz) easy-cook basmati rice in a saucepan of lightly salted boiling water for 15 minutes until tender, then drain. Meanwhile, boil 4 eggs in a saucepan of water for 6 minutes, then drain and cool under cold running water. Place 250 g (8 oz) smoked haddock in a microwave-proof dish, cover and cook in a microwave oven on high for 2–3 minutes. Skin and flake the haddock, discarding any bones.

Melt 15 g (½ oz) butter in a saucepan and cook ½ finely chopped onion over a gentle heat, stirring frequently, for about 3 minutes until softened. Add 2 teaspoons mild curry paste and cook, stirring, for 1–2 minutes. Add the cooked rice and fish, and season well. Stir over a medium heat for about 2 minutes until hot, then stir in 4 tablespoons chopped flat leaf parsley and the juice of ½ lemon. Peel the eggs, quarter and arrange on top of the kedgeree to serve.

Cherry Tomato and Cod Stir-Fry with Bacon

Serves 4

2 tablespoons olive oil

1 bunch of spring onions, trimmed and roughly chopped

1 garlic clove, thinly sliced

175 g (6 oz) rindless streaky bacon, chopped

250 g (8 oz) cherry tomatoes, halved

375 g (12 oz) skinless cod, coley or haddock fillet, cut into cubes

finely grated rind of 1 lemon

2 large handfuls of spinach leaves

150 g (5 oz) feta cheese, crumbled

warm crusty bread, to serve

- Heat the oil in a large, heavy-based pan frying pan and cook the spring onions, garlic and bacon over a high heat, stirring frequently, for 2–3 minutes until the onions are softened and the bacon is browned. Add the tomatoes and fish, reduce the heat and cook, stirring gently and tossing occasionally so that the fish cubes stay intact as much as possible, for 3–4 minutes until the fish is opaque and cooked through.

- Scatter over the lemon rind and spinach leaves, cover and cook for 1–2 minutes until the spinach has wilted, then gently fold the ingredients together. Scatter over the feta.

- Serve piled on to warmed serving plates with warm crusty bread to mop up the juices.

 Cod, Tomato and Bacon Gratin

Melt 15 g (½ oz) butter with 1 tablespoon olive oil in a frying pan and cook 1 bunch of trimmed and chopped spring onions and 6 chopped rindless smoked back bacon rashers over a high heat, stirring frequently, for 2 minutes. Add 375 g (12 oz) cubed skinless cod fillet and cook, stirring gently, for 2 minutes. Transfer to a flame-proof serving dish and sprinkle with 4 tablespoons breadcrumbs mixed with 2 tablespoons grated Cheddar cheese and 1 tablespoon chopped parsley. Top with a handful of halved cherry tomatoes. Cook under a high grill for 2 minutes. Serve with crusty French bread.

 Tomato and Smoked Cod Bake

Heat 1 tablespoon olive oil in a heavy-based frying pan and cook 4 trimmed, cleaned and sliced leeks, 1 sliced garlic clove and 175 g (6 oz) chopped rindless streaky bacon over a high heat, stirring frequently, for 3 minutes. Transfer to an ovenproof dish with 375 g (12 oz) cubed skinless smoked cod and 4 sliced beef tomatoes. Season with pepper and toss to mix. Toast 4 slices of white bread, then whizz in a processor to make breadcrumbs. In a small bowl, mix the breadcrumbs with 3 tablespoons grated Cheddar cheese and 1 tablespoon chopped parsley.

Sprinkle over the fish and place in a preheated oven, 180°C (350°F), Gas Mark 4, for 25 minutes. Serve with warm crusty bread.

30 Sticky Honey and Chilli Salmon Skewers with Rice

Serves 4

4 tablespoons sweet chilli sauce
4 tablespoons clear honey
4 tablespoons chopped coriander
2 spring onions, finely sliced
1 tablespoon sesame oil
500 g (1 lb) skinless salmon fillet,
   cut into chunks
salt and pepper

For the rice

250 g (8 oz) easy-cook basmati
   rice
2 tablespoons sesame oil
1 red onion, thinly sliced
6 spring onions, roughly chopped
175 g (6 oz) sugar snap peas,
   shredded
4 tablespoons chopped coriander

- Bring a saucepan of salted water to the boil and cook the rice for 15 minutes until just tender, then drain. Keep warm.

- Meanwhile, mix together the chilli sauce, honey, coriander, spring onions and oil in a large bowl. Add the salmon chunks and toss well to coat. Season with a little pepper.

- Thread the salmon on to 8 metal skewers. Place on a grill rack lined with foil and cook under a preheated medium grill for 7–8 minutes, turning 2–3 times, until lightly charred in places and cooked through.

- Meanwhile, heat the oil in a large wok or heavy-based frying pan and stir-fry the red onion over a high heat for 3 minutes. Add the spring onions and sugar snap peas and stir-fry for a further 2 minutes until just beginning to soften. Add the drained rice and stir-fry for 2 minutes, then add the coriander and toss well. Spoon the rice on to serving plates and arrange the hot salmon skewers on top.

 Honey and Mustard Salmon with Courgette Ribbons In a bowl, mix together 1 tablespoon each wholegrain mustard and light soy sauce, the juice of 1 lemon and 1 teaspoon clear honey. Place 4 salmon fillets on a foil-lined grill rack and brush over the honey mixture. Cook the salmon under a preheated medium-high grill for 8 minutes or until browned and cooked through. Remove and serve with steamed courgette ribbons and lemon wedges for squeezing over.

 Honey-Seared Salmon with Coriander Noodles Cook 200 g (7 oz) medium egg noodles in a saucepan of boiling water for about 4 minutes until tender. Drain and rinse under cold running water until cool, then drain again. Combine the noodles with 4 tablespoons each chopped fresh coriander, mint and basil and 2 trimmed and shredded courgettes. Add 2 tablespoons light soy sauce and 1 tablespoon lime juice and toss with the noodles to coat. Cut 500 g (1 lb) skinless salmon fillet into 1.5 cm (¾ inch) wide strips and toss with 2 tablespoons clear honey and pepper. Heat a large, nonstick frying pan over a high heat and cook the salmon for 2 minutes on each side or until the honey coating is browned. To serve, place the noodles on serving plates and top with the salmon strips.

30 Black Olive and Sunblush Tomato Risotto with Cod

Serves 4

4 pieces of cod loin, about 175 g (6 oz) each

2 tablespoons olive oil

1 red onion, finely chopped

100 g (3½ oz) pitted black olives, roughly chopped

100 g (3½ oz) sunblush tomatoes, roughly chopped

250 g (8 oz) Arborio risotto rice

900 ml (1½ pints) hot rich chicken stock

50 g (2 oz) Parmesan cheese, freshly grated

50 g (2 oz) basil, roughly chopped

pepper

- Place the cod pieces in a roasting tin and drizzle with 1 tablespoon of the oil. Season with pepper. Set aside.

- Heat the remaining tablespoon of oil in a large, heavy-based frying pan and cook the onion over a medium heat, stirring frequently, for 3–4 minutes until softened. Add the olives and tomatoes and cook, stirring, for 1 minute. Add the rice, then pour in half the stock. Bring to the boil, then reduce the heat and simmer gently, stirring occasionally, for 5–6 minutes until almost all the stock has been absorbed.

- Place the cod in a preheated oven, 200°C (400°F), Gas Mark 6, for 15 minutes until cooked through. Meanwhile, stir the remaining stock into the rice and continue simmering, stirring occasionally, until almost all the stock has been absorbed and the rice is tender. Remove from the heat and stir in the Parmesan and basil. Season with pepper.

- Serve the risotto on warmed serving plates with the roasted cod on top.

---

 1 Parmesan Cod Fillets with Avocado and Cress Salad Place 4 tablespoons plain flour in a shallow dish and season with salt and pepper. Dust 4 cod fillets, about 150 g (5 oz) each, with the seasoned flour, then dip the fish into 2 eggs beaten in a shallow bowl and finally dust with 75 g (3 oz) finely grated Parmesan cheese, making sure that the fish is well covered. Heat 1 tablespoon olive oil in large, heavy-based frying pan and cook the cod fillets over a high heat for 2 minutes on each side, depending on their thickness, until browned and cooked through. Meanwhile, toss together 2 stoned, peeled and sliced ripe avocados and 1 punnet cress with 2 tablespoons extra virgin olive oil and the juice of 1 lemon. Serve with the cod fillets.

2 Cod with Sunblush Tomatoes, Basil and Mozzarella Place 4 pieces of cod loin, about 175 g (6 oz) each, in an oiled roasting tin. Drizzle with olive oil and season with salt and pepper. Top with 100 g (3½ oz) roughly chopped sunblush tomatoes, 50 g (2 oz) chopped basil and 2 finely sliced balls of mozzarella, about 150 g (5 oz). Sprinkle over 50 g (2 oz) grated Parmesan cheese, drizzle with more olive oil and place on the top shelf of a preheated oven, 220°C (425°F), Gas Mark 7, for 15 minutes until golden.

QuickCook

Fast and Veggie

Recipes listed by cooking time

30

20

10

Thai Vegetable Curry

Serves 4

500 g (1 lb) butternut squash, peeled, deseeded and cut into chunks

2 red peppers, cored, deseeded and cut into chunks

175 g (6 oz) baby corn, halved

250 g (8 oz) cauliflower florets

2 tablespoons Thai green curry paste

2 x 400 g (13 oz) cans coconut milk

150 ml (¼ pint) vegetable stock

175 g (6 oz) sugar snap peas

2 tablespoons cold water

1 tablespoon cornflour

4 tablespoons chopped fresh coriander

cooked Thai jasmine rice, to serve

- Place the squash, red peppers, corn and cauliflower in a large, heavy-based saucepan, add the curry paste, coconut milk and stock and bring to the boil. Reduce the heat, cover with a lid and simmer for 15 minutes until the vegetables are tender, adding the sugar snap peas for the final 5 minutes of cooking.

- Blend the measurement water with the cornflour, add to the curry and cook, stirring constantly, until it thickens slightly. Stir in the coriander and serve with Thai Jasmine rice, if liked.

Thai Corn and Cauliflower Curried Soup Dice 250 g (8 oz) cauliflower florets and place in a large, heavy-based saucepan with 2 x 400 g (13 oz) cans coconut milk, 2 tablespoons Thai green curry paste, 150 ml (¼ pint) vegetable stock and 175 g (6 oz) halved baby corn. Cook, stirring occasionally, for 9 minutes over a high heat. Stir in 4 tablespoons chopped fresh coriander before serving.

Malaysian Vegetable Curry In a food processor, combine 3 garlic cloves, 2 red chillies, 2 lemon grass stalks, a 3.5 cm (1½ inch) piece of fresh root ginger, peeled, 3 chopped shallots, 3 tablespoons groundnut oil, 1 tablespoon palm sugar and 1 teaspoon each ground turmeric and ground cinnamon to make a curry paste. Place 500 g (1 lb) butternut squash, peeled, deseeded and cut into chunks, 2 red peppers, cut into chunks, 175 g (6 oz) halved baby corn and 250 g (8 oz) cauliflower florets in a large, heavy-based saucepan, add the curry paste, 2 star anise, 2 dried kaffir lime leaves, 2 x 400 g (13 oz) cans coconut milk and 150 ml (¼ pint) vegetable stock and bring to the boil. Reduce the heat, cover and simmer for 15 minutes until the vegetables are tender, adding 175 g (6 oz) sugar snap peas for the final 5 minutes. Blend 2 tablespoons cold water with 1 tablespoon cornflour, add to the curry and cook, stirring constantly, until it thickens slightly. Stir in 4 tablespoons chopped fresh coriander and serve with cooked Thai jasmine rice, if liked.

FAM-FAST-QIZ

3⃝ Spicy Bean Burgers with Tomato Salsa

Serves 4

400 g (13 oz) can red kidney beans
4 tablespoons chopped coriander
1 small red chilli, finely chopped
1 tablespoon ground paprika
½ teaspoon ground cumin
½ teaspoon ground coriander
3 spring onions, chopped
1 egg yolk
100 g (3½ oz) white breadcrumbs
vegetable oil, for shallow-frying

For the salsa

2 tomatoes, finely chopped
1 tablespoon olive oil
2 tablespoons chopped coriander
2 spring onions, roughly chopped
pepper

To serve

4 soft wholemeal rolls
rocket leaves

- Drain the kidney beans and place in a bowl and mash with a fork until soft but still retaining some bean shapes. Add the coriander, half the chilli, the ground spices, spring onions, egg yolk and breadcrumbs and mix well. Form into 4 patties.

- Heat 3–4 tablespoons vegetable oil in a large, heavy-based frying pan and cook the burgers over a medium-high heat for 2–3 minutes on each side until browned. Keep warm while making the salsa.

- For the salsa, place the tomatoes, olive oil and coriander in a bowl, add the remaining chilli and the spring onions and stir well to mix. Season with a little pepper.

- Serve each burger in a soft wholemeal roll with a few rocket leaves and some of the tomato salsa.

 Quick Bean and Pasta Soup

Place a drained 400 g (13 oz) can mixed beans in a saucepan along with 300 g (10 oz) shop-bought tomato-based pasta sauce and 750 ml (1¼ pints) hot vegetable stock. Bring to the boil, then stir in 100 g (3½ oz) dried mini pasta shapes of your choice and cook according to the packet instructions until just tender. Serve with some warm crusty bread rolls.

 Tortilla Bean Cheesecake

Heat 1 teaspoon olive oil in a large saucepan and cook 1 chopped onion over a medium heat, stirring frequently, for 3 minutes. Stir in ½ teaspoon chilli powder and a 400 g (13 oz) can chopped tomatoes with herbs, then cook over a high heat for 5 minutes until slightly thickened. Add 200 g (7 oz) frozen mixed vegetables and cook for a further 3 minutes. Stir through a drained 400 g (13 oz) can red kidney beans. Take 5 soft flour tortillas and place one on a heatproof plate, spread with a little of the sauce and sprinkle over a handful of grated Cheddar cheese. Continue layering the tortillas, sauce and cheese, finishing with a sprinkling of cheese. Set the plate on a baking sheet and place in a preheated oven, 180°C (350°F), Gas Mark 4, for 10 minutes until the cheese has melted. Cut into wedges and serve with soured cream and chopped spring onions.

30 Roasted Vegetable Pasta with Garlic and Herb Sauce

Serves 4

2 courgettes, trimmed and cut into chunks

1 aubergine, trimmed and cut into chunks

1 large red onion, cut into chunks

4 tablespoons olive oil

1 large onion, chopped

2 garlic cloves, sliced

500 g (1 lb) tomatoes, roughly chopped

3 tablespoons tomato purée

4 tablespoons chopped parsley

1 tablespoon chopped rosemary leaves

150 ml (¼ pint) water

250 g (8 oz) dried fusilli

salt

warm crusty bread, to serve (optional)

- Place the courgettes, aubergine and onion in a large roasting tin and toss with 3 tablespoons of the olive oil. Place in a preheated oven, 220°C (425°F), Gas Mark 7, for 20 minutes until tender and lightly charred in places.

- Meanwhile, heat the remaining tablespoon of oil in a large, heavy-based frying pan and cook the onion and garlic over a medium-high heat, stirring frequently, for 3 minutes until softened. Add the tomatoes and cook, stirring occasionally, for a further 10 minutes. Add the tomato purée, herbs and measurement water and bring to the boil, then reduce the heat and simmer for 5 minutes.

- While the sauce is cooking, bring a large saucepan of lightly salted water to the boil and cook the fusilli for 10–12 minutes until just tender, then drain.

- Add the roasted vegetables to the tomato sauce along with the drained pasta and toss well together. Serve in warmed serving bowls, with warm crusty bread, if liked.

 Creamy Roasted Vegetable Pasta

Cook 500 g (1 lb) fresh fusilli in a large saucepan of lightly salted boiling water for 3–4 minutes or until just tender. Drain, return to the pan and stir in 300 g (10 oz) shop-bought roasted vegetable pasta sauce, a 300 g (10 oz) jar artichoke antipasti, drained well, and 1 tablespoon chopped rosemary leaves. Heat through over a medium heat. Serve immediately, sprinkled with freshly grated Parmesan cheese, with garlic bread.

 Roasted Vegetable Couscous with Feta

Place 2 courgettes and 1 aubergine, each trimmed and cut into chunks, and 1 large red onion, cut into chunks, in a large roasting tin and toss with 3 tablespoons olive oil. Place in a preheated oven, 220°C (425°F), Gas Mark 7, for 20 minutes until tender and lightly charred in places. Meanwhile, place 200 g (7 oz) couscous in a bowl and add enough warm water to cover by 1 cm (½ inch). Mix in ½ teaspoon salt and leave the couscous to absorb the water for 15 minutes. Fluff up the couscous with a fork and mix in 1 tablespoon olive oil and the juice of ½ lemon. Stir in the roasted vegetables and season with salt and pepper, then crumble over 200 g (7 oz) feta cheese and scatter with some shredded basil.

 # Egg, Basil and Cheese Salad with Cherry Tomatoes

Serves 4

2 tablespoons olive oil

2 eggs, beaten

25 g (1 oz) basil, roughly chopped

200 g (7 oz) feta cheese, drained and crumbled

250 g (8 oz) cherry plum tomatoes, halved

80 g (3 oz) watercress

1 tablespoon balsamic vinegar

pepper

- Heat 1 tablespoon of the oil in a 25 cm (10 inch) nonstick frying pan and swirl around. Beat the eggs in a large jug with the basil and plenty of pepper, then pour into the pan in a thin layer and cook for 1–2 minutes until golden and set. Remove and cut into thick strips.

- Meanwhile, toss the feta and cherry tomatoes with the watercress in a serving bowl. Mix the remaining oil with the balsamic vinegar, pour over the salad and toss to coat.

- Add the omelette strips, toss to mix and serve while still warm.

 Cheese, Cherry Tomato and Basil Frittata Heat 2 tablespoons olive oil in a 25 cm (10 inch) heavy-based frying pan and swirl around. Beat 6 eggs in a jug and season well, then pour into the pan and cook over a medium heat for 2–3 minutes. Scatter over 250 g (8 oz) halved cherry tomatoes, 200 g (7 oz) feta cheese, drained and crumbled, and a handful of pitted black olives. Cook for a further 3 minutes until the base is set, then place under a preheated high grill, making sure that the pan handle is turned away from the heat, and cook for a further 2–3 minutes until the top is set and the feta has softened a little.

Serve with a handful of rocket leaves and a snipped basil leaves scattered over the top. Drizzle with lemon juice and serve in wedges.

Basil, Egg and Cheese Pizza with Cherry Tomatoes Make up a 150 g (5 oz) packet pizza base mix according to the packet instructions and roll out to a 25 cm (10 inch) round on a large baking sheet. Spread with 8 tablespoons shop-bought pizza topping sauce and scatter with 100 g (3½ oz) halved cherry tomatoes, leaving a well in the centre, then break an egg into the well. Scatter with a handful of basil leaves and 75 g (3 oz) ready-grated mozzarella cheese, avoiding the egg. Place in a preheated oven, 220°C (425°F), Gas Mark 7, for 15–20 minutes until the base is browned and crisp and the cheese has melted.

Sweet Potato, Chickpea and Cashew Curry

Serves 4

2 tablespoons vegetable oil

1 onion, chopped

4 sweet potatoes, peeled and chopped

3 tablespoons korma curry paste

400 g (13 oz) can chickpeas, drained

400 g (13 oz) can chopped tomatoes

400 g (13 oz) can coconut milk

100 g (3½ oz) toasted cashew nuts

3 tablespoons chopped fresh coriander

warm naan breads or cooked rice, to serve (optional)

- Heat the oil in a large, deep heavy-based frying pan and cook the onion and sweet potatoes over a medium heat, stirring occasionally, for 5 minutes until softened. Add the curry paste and cook, stirring, for 1 minute, then add the chickpeas, tomatoes and coconut milk and bring to the boil.

- Reduce the heat and simmer for 10 minutes until the sauce has thickened slightly and the potatoes are tender. Stir in half the cashew nuts.

- Serve, garnished with the coriander and remaining cashew nuts, with warm naan breads or cooked rice, if liked.

 Sweet Potato, Chickpea and Cashew Couscous Add boiling water to a 200 g (7 oz) packet instant roasted vegetable-flavoured couscous, following the packet instructions, and leave to absorb the water for 5 minutes. Meanwhile, heat 2 tablespoons vegetable oil in a large, deep frying pan and cook 1 chopped onion and 4 peeled and chopped sweet potatoes over a medium heat, stirring occasionally, for 5 minutes until softened. Add a drained 400 g (13 oz) can chickpeas and heat through. Stir into the couscous with 3 tablespoons chopped coriander and 125 g (4 oz) toasted cashew nuts.

 Luxury Sweet Potato, Chickpea and Cashew Korma In a food processor, whizz 50 g (2 oz) whole blanched almonds with 2 garlic cloves until finely ground and like a paste. Heat 2 tablespoons vegetable oil in a large, deep frying pan and cook 1 chopped onion with 4 peeled and chopped sweet potatoes and 3 tablespoons korma curry paste over a medium heat, stirring occasionally, for 5 minutes until the vegetables are softened. Add the almond mixture and cook, stirring, for a further 2 minutes, then add a 400 g (13 oz) can chickpeas, drained, and a 400 g (13 oz) can chopped tomatoes, two-thirds of a 400 g (13 oz) can coconut milk and 125 ml (4 fl oz) double cream. Bring almost to the boil, then reduce the heat and simmer for 10 minutes until the sauce has thickened slightly and the potatoes are tender. Stir in 50 g (2 oz) toasted cashew nuts. Serve scattered with 3 tablespoons chopped fresh coriander and an extra 50 g (2 oz) toasted cashew nuts, with warm naan breads or cooked rice, if liked.

30 Lemon Mixed Vegetable Kebabs with Nut Pilaff

Serves 4

250 g (8 oz) easy-cook brown rice

1 aubergine, cut into chunks

2 courgettes cut into chunks

200 g (7 oz) chestnut
mushrooms, halved if large

4 tablespoons flat leaf parsley,
plus extra to serve

1 tablespoon rosemary leaves

150 ml (¼ pint) olive oil

grated rind and juice of 2 lemons

250 g (8 oz) cherry tomatoes

100 g (3½ oz) toasted flaked
almonds

2 carrots, peeled and grated

2 tablespoons light soy sauce

salt and pepper

- For the pilaff, bring a large saucepan of lightly salted water to the boil and cook the rice for 25 minutes until tender. Drain and refresh under cold running water, then drain again.

- Meanwhile, place the aubergine, courgettes and mushrooms in a large bowl. Chop the 4 tablespoons of parsley and the rosemary, and whisk together with the olive oil, lemon rind and juice in a jug. Season with pepper, then pour over the vegetables and toss together.

- Thread the dressed vegetables with the tomatoes on to 8 metal skewers. Cook the skewers under a preheated medium grill or over a barbecue, turning occasionally, for 8–10 minutes until lightly charred and tender.

- Toss the cooled rice with the almonds, carrots, the remaining parsley and soy sauce. Season with a little pepper. Serve the hot kebabs on a bed of the rice salad.

 Egg-Fried Rice with Mixed Vegetables

Beat 2 eggs in a bowl. Heat 1 tablespoon vegetable oil in a large frying pan, pour in the eggs in a thin layer and cook over a medium heat for 1–2 minutes until golden and set. Remove and shred. Heat another tablespoon of oil in the pan and stir-fry 300 g (10 oz) frozen mixed stir-fry vegetables for 3–4 minutes. Add 250 g (8 oz) ready-cooked long-grain rice and the shredded omelette and toss. Season with light soy sauce to taste and serve with 50 g (2 oz) toasted flaked almonds.

 Lemon Mixed Vegetable Kebabs with Minted Couscous

Prepare the vegetable kebabs as above. Place 200 g (7 oz) couscous in a bowl and add enough boiling water to cover by 1 cm (½ inch). Leave to absorb the water while cooking the kebabs as above. Whisk together 3 tablespoons olive oil, 2 tablespoons lemon juice, 1 tablespoon clear honey, ½ teaspoon harissa paste and a handful of chopped mint in a jug, then pour over the couscous and toss well to coat. Serve with the hot kebabs.

Mixed Mushroom Stroganoff

Serves 4

4 tablespoons olive oil

1 onion, finely chopped

375 g (12 oz) chestnut mushrooms, trimmed and quartered

175 g (6 oz) shiitake mushrooms, trimmed and halved

100 g (3½ oz) oyster mushrooms, trimmed and halved

1 tablespoon brandy

1 teaspoon Dijon mustard

200 ml (7 fl oz) crème fraîche

pepper

cooked brown or white long-grain rice, to serve

4 tablespoons chopped parsley

- Heat the oil in a large, heavy-based frying pan and cook the onion over a medium heat, stirring frequently, for 2–3 minutes until softened. Add the chestnut mushrooms and cook, stirring frequently, for 5 minutes until lightly browned. Add the shiitake and oyster mushrooms and cook, stirring frequently, for 5 minutes until softened.

- Pour the brandy into the mushroom mixture and stir over a high heat until evaporated. Mix the mustard into the crème fraîche, then spoon into the pan and heat for 2 minutes until piping hot. Season well with pepper.

- Serve the stroganoff over cooked brown or white long-grain rice, with the parsley scattered over.

 Mushroom Stroganoff on Wholegrain Toast

Thickly slice 250 g (8 oz) trimmed chestnut mushrooms and 250 g (8 oz) trimmed portobello mushrooms. Melt 25 g (1 oz) garlic butter in a large frying pan, add the mushrooms and cook over a high heat, stirring frequently, for 4–5 minutes. Meanwhile, toast and butter 4 thick slices of wholegrain bread. Stir 1 tablespoon wholegrain mustard and 300 ml (½ pint) soured cream into the mushrooms. Season to taste and serve on the toast with 1 tablespoon chopped chives scattered over.

 Pepper, Mustard and Mushroom Stroganoff Melt 25 g (1 oz) butter in a large frying pan with 2 teaspoons olive oil. Add 1 trimmed, cleaned and thinly sliced leek and 1 red and 1 green cored, deseeded and sliced pepper and cook over a medium heat, stirring occasionally, for 5 minutes. Add 375 g (12 oz) trimmed and quartered chestnut mushrooms, 175 g (6 oz) trimmed and halved shiitake mushrooms and 100 g (3½ oz) trimmed and halved oyster mushrooms and cook, stirring frequently, for 3 minutes. Transfer to a plate. Add 150 ml (¼ pint) dry white wine to the pan, bring to the boil and continue boiling for 2–3 minutes until reduced by half. Meanwhile, stir 4 teaspoons wholegrain mustard and 2 teaspoons prepared English mustard into 400 ml (14 fl oz) crème fraîche. Add to the pan and stir, then return the vegetables. Gently heat for 2 minutes, then stir in 4 tablespoons chopped flat leaf parsley and season with pepper. Serve on a bed of cooked rice or with creamy mashed potato.

20 Quesadillas with Refried Beans and Avocado Salsa

Serves 4

1 tablespoon olive oil, plus extra
1 bunch of spring onions, chopped
½ teaspoon ground cumin
½ teaspoon ground coriander
½ teaspoon ground paprika
435 g (14¼ oz) can refried beans
200 g (7 oz) can red kidney
   beans, drained and rinsed
8 soft flour tortillas
175 g (6 oz) Cheddar cheese, grated

For the salsa

2 vine-ripened tomatoes, chopped
1 ripe avocado, stoned, peeled
   and roughly chopped
3 tablespoons chopped coriander
1 tablespoon olive oil
pepper

- Heat the oil in a large, heavy-based frying pan and cook the spring onions over a high heat, stirring frequently, for 2 minutes. Add all the spices and cook, stirring, for 1 minute. Add the refried beans and kidney beans and cook, stirring, for 2–3 minutes until piping hot, adding 2 tablespoons water to loosen if necessary.

- Divide the mixture between the flour tortillas. Fold each tortilla into quarters to encompass the filling, transfer to a lightly oiled ovenproof dish and scatter over the Cheddar.

- Cook under a preheated medium grill for 5–10 minutes until the cheese has melted and the quesadillas are piping hot. Meanwhile, mix all the ingredients for the salsa together and season with pepper.

- Serve 2 quesadillas on each of 4 warmed serving plates and spoon over the salsa.

 Quick and Easy Quesadillas with Refried Beans Heat 1 tablespoon olive oil in a large, heavy-based frying pan and cook 1 bunch of trimmed and roughly chopped spring onions over a high heat, stirring frequently, for 2 minutes. Add ½ teaspoon each ground cumin and coriander and paprika, and cook, stirring, for 1 minute. Add a 435 g (14¼ oz) can refried beans and cook, stirring, for 2–3 minutes until piping hot, adding 2 tablespoons water to loosen if necessary. Divide the bean mixture and 75 g (3 oz) grated Cheddar cheese between 8 soft flour tortillas and add a spoonful of shop-bought salsa to each. Fold each tortilla into quarters to encompass the filling, place on a foil-lined grill rack, spaced apart, and scatter over another 75 g (3 oz) grated Cheddar cheese. Warm under a preheated medium grill for 2 minutes. Scatter with chopped coriander to serve.

Quesadillas with Homemade Refried Beans Heat 2 tablespoons olive oil in a large frying pan and cook 1 chopped onion and 1 roughly chopped small red chilli over a medium heat, stirring, for 5 minutes until softened. Add a drained 400 g (13 oz) can borlotti beans and cook, stirring, for 2 minutes. Transfer to a food processor with a large handful of coriander and blend but retaining some texture from the beans. Follow the recipe above, using the homemade refried beans in place of the canned refried beans.

30   Goats' Cheese and Spinach Risotto

Serves 4

1 tablespoon olive oil
1 large onion, thinly sliced
1 garlic clove, chopped
250 g (8 oz) Arborio risotto rice
900 ml (1½ pints) hot vegetable
  stock
300 g (10 oz) spinach leaves
finely grated rind and juice of
  1 lemon
175 g (6 oz) rinded goats' cheese,
  roughly chopped into cubes
pepper
freshly grated Parmesan cheese,
  to serve

- Heat the oil in a large, heavy-based frying pan and cook the onion and garlic over a medium heat, stirring occasionally, for 3–4 minutes until softened.

- Add the rice and cook, stirring, for 1 minute. Add half the stock and bring to the boil, then reduce the heat and simmer gently, stirring occasionally, for 5–6 minutes until almost all the stock has been absorbed. Add the remaining stock and continue simmering, stirring occasionally, until the rice is tender and almost all the stock has been absorbed. Add the spinach leaves and lemon rind and juice, and cook, stirring, for 2–3 minutes until the spinach has wilted and is well mixed through the rice.

- Scatter over the cheese and then stir through the risotto until almost melted yet still retaining some of its shape. Spoon into warmed serving bowls and serve with grated Parmesan and a good grinding of pepper.

 10 Tagliatelle with Goats' Cheese and Spinach Bring a large saucepan of lightly salted water to the boil and cook 500 g (1 lb) fresh tagliatelle for 3–4 minutes or until just tender. Meanwhile, heat through 300 g (10 oz) ready-made tomato pasta sauce in a saucepan. Drain the pasta and return to the pan. Toss in the sauce, add 300 g (10 oz) spinach leaves and stir over a medium heat until the spinach wilts into the sauce. Serve with 100 g (3½ oz) goats' cheese crumbled over the top and some freshly grated Parmesan cheese.

 20 Goats' Cheese and Spinach Pizza Spread each of 4 shop-bought ready-made pizza bases with 1 tablespoon tomato purée. Heat a large saucepan over a medium heat, add 300 g (10 oz) spinach leaves and heat until wilted, making sure that the spinach doesn't catch on the bottom of the pan. Arrange 175 g (6 oz) rinded goats' cheese, roughly chopped into cubes, and the spinach on the pizza bases, then grate 75 g (3 oz) Parmesan cheese over the top. Drizzle with olive oil and place in a preheated oven, 200°C (400°F), Gas Mark 6, for 10 minutes until the base is lightly browned. Serve with a green salad.

Tomato, Rosemary and Cannellini Bean Stew

Serves 4

3 tablespoons olive oil

1 large red onion, sliced

2 teaspoons garlic purée

2 tablespoons chopped rosemary leaves

2 x 400 g (13 oz) cans cannellini beans, drained

500 g (1 lb) jar tomato pasta sauce

wholemeal crusty bread, to serve

- Heat the oil in a large, heavy-based frying pan and cook the onion over a medium heat, stirring occasionally, for 2 minutes. Add the garlic purée and rosemary and cook, stirring constantly, for 30 seconds.

- Add the beans and tomato sauce and bring to the boil. Reduce the heat, cover and simmer for 6–7 minutes until piping hot.

- Serve with fresh, torn wholemeal bread for mopping up the juices.

 Vegetarian Haricot Bean Cassoulet

Heat 3 tablespoons olive oil in a large, heavy-based frying pan and cook 1 small chopped onion, 2 peeled and diced carrots and 1 tablespoon chopped rosemary leaves over a medium heat, stirring occasionally, for 3–4 minutes until softened. Add 2 x 400 g (13 oz) cans haricot beans, drained, with 600 ml (1 pint) vegetable stock and bring to the boil. Simmer briskly, uncovered, for 10 minutes until piping hot, then place a third of the beans into a food processor and whizz until smooth. Return the puréed beans to the pan, stir and heat through briefly. Season with salt and pepper, then serve with crusty bread.

 Vegetarian Sausage and Butter Bean

Stew Heat 2 tablespoons olive oil in a large, deep heavy-based frying pan and cook 8 good-quality thick vegetarian sausages over a medium heat, turning frequently, for 8–10 minutes until browned and cooked through. Add 2 red onions, cut into slim wedges, and cook, stirring frequently, for 5 minutes until softened. Add 2 x 400 g (13 oz) cans each butter beans, drained, and chopped tomatoes with 4 tablespoons sun-dried tomato paste. Bring to the boil and simmer briskly, uncovered and stirring occasionally, for 10 minutes until the sauce is thick and pulpy. Serve in warmed serving bowls with plenty of chopped parsley scattered over.

30 Grilled Haloumi with Warm Couscous Salad

Serves 4

200 g (7 oz) couscous
½ teaspoon salt
5 tablespoons olive oil
2 red onions, thinly sliced
1 red chilli, roughly chopped
400 g (13 oz) can chickpeas, drained
175 g (6 oz) cherry tomatoes, halved
3 tablespoons chopped parsley
1 tablespoon thyme leaves
375 g (12 oz) haloumi cheese, thickly sliced

- Place the couscous in a bowl and add enough warm water to cover by 1 cm (½ inch). Mix in the salt and leave the couscous to absorb the water for 20 minutes.

- Meanwhile, heat 3 tablespoons of the oil in a large frying pan and cook the onions and two-thirds of the chilli over a medium heat, stirring, for 4–5 minutes until softened. Add the chickpeas and tomatoes and cook over a high heat, stirring occasionally, for 3 minutes until the chickpeas are heated through and the tomatoes are softened but still retaining their shape.

- Meanwhile, mix the remaining olive oil and chilli with the herbs in a shallow bowl. Add the haloumi slices and toss to coat. Place the haloumi slices on a grill rack lined with foil and cook under a hot grill for 2–3 minutes until browned in places.

- Stir the couscous into the chickpea mixture and cook for 1 minute to heat through. Serve piled on to warmed serving plates, topped with the haloumi slices.

---

10 Quick Haloumi with Chilli

Mix 2 chopped red chillies with 2 tablespoons extra virgin olive oil and leave to infuse while cooking the haloumi. Heat a nonstick frying pan over a high heat. Cut 375 g (12 oz) haloumi cheese into medium slices. Cook the haloumi slices in batches for 2 minutes on each side until browned in places. When all the pieces are cooked, place a handful of salad leaves on each of 4 serving plates and top with the haloumi slices. Give the chilli oil a stir, spoon it over the haloumi and finish with a squeeze of lemon juice.

20 Haloumi Cheese Kebabs with Couscous

Place 200 g (7 oz) couscous in a bowl and add enough warm water to cover by 1 cm (½ inch). Mix in ½ teaspoon salt and leave the couscous to swell and absorb the water for 20 minutes. Meanwhile, in a small bowl, mix together 3 tablespoons olive oil, 1 crushed garlic clove, 1 teaspoon each fresh thyme leaves and chopped oregano, rosemary and mint, the juice of 1 lime and salt and pepper. Place 375 g (12 oz) haloumi cheese, cut into 2.5 cm (1 inch) cubes, and 8 trimmed chestnut mushrooms in a separate non-metallic bowl, pour over the marinade and mix to coat evenly. Cover and leave to marinate until you are ready to cook. Divide the cheese, mushrooms and 8 cherry tomatoes evenly between 4 metal skewers, or bamboo skewers presoaked in cold water for 30 minutes. Cook over a barbecue or under a preheated high grill for 5–6 minutes until tinged brown at the edges, brushing any remaining marinade over the kebabs while they cook. Serve the kebabs with shop-bought salsa and the couscous.

 # Penne with Pan-Fried Butternut Squash and Pesto

Serves 4

500 g (1 lb) fresh penne
2 tablespoons olive oil
25 g (1 oz) butter
500 g (1 lb) ready-prepared
   butternut squash cubes or
   wedges
200 g (7 oz) green pesto
salt

- Bring a large saucepan of lightly salted water to the boil and cook the penne for 3 minutes or until just tender. Drain, return to the pan and toss with 1 tablespoon of the olive oil.

- Meanwhile, melt the butter with the remaining tablespoon of oil in a large, heavy-based frying pan or wok and cook the squash over a medium heat, turning frequently, for 7–8 minutes until softened and golden, covering for the final 3 minutes of cooking to enable the steam to cook the squash.

- Add the pasta and pesto to the squash and toss all the ingredients together for 1 minute to heat through. Serve in warmed serving bowls.

 Warm Butternut, Penne, Bacon and Camembert Salad Cook the butternut squash as above. Meanwhile, cook 200 g (7 oz) dried penne in a saucepan of salted boiling water for 10–12 minutes until just tender, then drain. Grill 8 rindless streaky bacon rashers until browned and crisp. Snip into pieces, add to the squash with the pasta and toss. Heat a frying pan and cook 75 g (3 oz) pine nuts over a medium-high heat, shaking the pan, for 3–4 minutes until toasted. Place all the ingredients in a bowl with 100 g (3½ oz) cubed Camembert and 150 g (5 oz) mixed salad leaves. Whisk together 2 tablespoons olive oil, 1 tablespoon green pesto and the juice of ½ lemon. Toss with the salad.

Summery Penne and Butternut Bake Bring a large saucepan of lightly salted water to the boil and cook 500 g (1 lb) fresh penne for 3 minutes or until just tender. Drain, return to the pan and toss with 1 tablespoon olive oil. Melt 25 g (1 oz) butter with 1 tablespoon olive oil in a large, heavy-based frying pan or wok and cook 500 g (1 lb) ready-prepared butternut squash cubes or wedges over a medium heat, turning frequently, for 7–8 minutes until softened and golden, covering for the final 3 minutes and adding 250 g (8 oz) peas, defrosted if frozen, for the final 1 minute of cooking. Add 2 x 200 ml (7 fl oz) cartons crème fraîche, the finely grated rind of 1 lemon and 4 tablespoons green pesto and toss well, then crumble in 200 g (7 oz) feta cheese and 200 g (7 oz) baby spinach leaves. Heat, stirring, for 2 minutes until the sauce is hot and the spinach wilted. Toss with the pasta, pile into a large, shallow gratin dish and scatter with 6 tablespoons freshly grated Parmesan cheese. Cook under a preheated high grill for 3–4 minutes until golden and bubbling.

10 Ciabatta Toasties with Mediterranean Vegetables

Serves 4

5 tablespoons olive oil, plus extra
 for drizzling
½ aubergine, trimmed and thinly
 sliced
1 ciabatta loaf
4 tablespoons green pesto
1 large beef tomato, thinly sliced
4 slices of mozzarella cheese
pepper

- Heat the oil in a large, heavy-based frying pan and cook the aubergine slices in batches over a high heat for 1–2 minutes on each side until browned and tender. Remove with a fish slice and keep warm.

- Meanwhile, cut the ciabatta loaf in half lengthways, then each half in half again widthways. Place on the grill rack and cook under a preheated high grill, cut-side up, for 1 minute until golden.

- Spread each ciabatta toastie with 1 tablespoon of the pesto. Top with the warm aubergine slices, then the tomato slices and finally the mozzarella slices. Drizzle each toastie with 1 tablespoon olive oil, then return to the grill and cook for a further 2 minutes until the mozzarella is melting and beginning to brown in places.

- Season with pepper and serve warm.

2 Mediterranean Ciabatta Pizzas

Halve a ciabatta loaf lengthways, then cut each half in half again widthways. Place all 4 pieces on a baking sheet. Heat 4 tablespoons olive oil in a large, heavy-based frying pan and cook ½ aubergine, trimmed and cut into cubes, over a high heat, tossing frequently, for 5 minutes until browned and tender. Spread each of the ciabatta pieces with 2 tablespoons sun-dried tomato paste, then top with 1 sliced beef tomato. Divide the aubergine between the ciabatta pieces. Slice 150 g (5 oz) mozzarella cheese and arrange over the top of the aubergine. Spoon 2 teaspoons green pesto over the top of each ciabatta piece, then cook under a preheated high grill for 5 minutes until the tops are melted and golden.

3 Mediterranean Vegetable Gratin

Heat 4 tablespoons olive oil in a large frying pan and cook 1 sliced aubergine in batches over a high heat for 1–2 minutes on each side until browned and tender. Loosely layer in a large, shallow gratin dish with 3 sliced large beef tomatoes, 2 x 150 g (5 oz) packs mozzarella cheese, drained and thinly sliced, and 6 tablespoons green pesto, seasoning between the layers. Scatter with 3 tablespoons freshly grated Parmesan cheese and cook under a preheated high grill for 8–10 minutes until golden and bubbling.

30 Fruity Chickpea Tagine with Coriander Couscous

Serves 4

200 g (7 oz) couscous
½ teaspoon salt
4 tablespoons olive oil
1 aubergine, cut into cubes
1 red onion, cut into chunks
2 red peppers, cut into chunks
1 tablespoon harissa paste
2 garlic cloves, chopped
2.5 cm (1 inch) piece of fresh root
   ginger, peeled and chopped
1 cinnamon stick
400 g (13 oz) can chickpeas,
   drained
400 g (13 oz) can chopped
   tomatoes
300 ml (½ pint) vegetable stock
1 tablespoon tomato purée
1 teaspoon sugar
100 g (3½ oz) ready-to-eat dried
   apricots, roughly chopped
50 g (2 oz) ready-to-eat dried
   prunes, roughly chopped
4 tablespoons chopped fresh
   coriander, plus extra to garnish

- Place the couscous in a bowl and add enough warm water to cover by 1 cm (½ inch). Mix in the salt and leave the couscous to absorb the water while making the tagine.

- Heat 2 tablespoons of the oil in a large, heavy-based frying pan and cook the aubergine over a medium heat, stirring occasionally, for 5 minutes. Add the onion and red peppers and cook, stirring occasionally, for a further 5 minutes. Stir in the harissa paste, garlic and ginger and cook, stirring, for a further 2 minutes. Add the cinnamon stick, chickpeas, tomatoes, stock, tomato purée, sugar and dried fruit and bring to the boil. Reduce the heat, cover and simmer for 10–15 minutes until all the vegetables are tender.

- Toss the couscous with the remaining 2 tablespoons oil, fluffing up with a fork. Stir in the chopped fresh coriander. Serve with the tagine, sprinkling each plate with extra chopped fresh coriander.

 Chickpea and Hummus Pitta Pockets Lightly toast 4 pitta breads. Cut each pitta in half to form 2 pockets. Place 1 tablespoon shop-bought chickpea hummus in each pocket together with 1 grated large carrot and ¼ chopped cucumber. Serve immediately.

 Chickpea, Tomato and Feta Salad Finely slice 1 red onion and 2 red chillies, then toss with 250 g (8 oz) roughly chopped tomatoes in a large salad bowl. Dress with the juice of 1½ lemons and about 6 tablespoons extra virgin olive oil. Season with salt and pepper. Warm through a drained 400 g (13 oz) can chickpeas in a saucepan with 4 tablespoons water, then add about 90% to the bowl. Mash the remaining whole beans with a fork, then add to the bowl and toss all the ingredients to mix well. Leave to stand for the flavours to mingle for 5 minutes, then crumble over 200 g (7 oz) feta cheese and scatter with some torn mint and basil leaves.

30 Spinach, Pine Nut and Cheese Filo Pie

Serves 4

1 tablespoon olive oil

1 onion, roughly chopped

1 garlic clove, thinly sliced

75 g (3 oz) pine nuts, toasted

1 kg (2 lb) frozen spinach, defrosted and well drained

2 eggs

2 egg yolks

2 x 200 g (7 oz) packs feta cheese, drained and crumbled

2 teaspoons ground nutmeg

6 sheets of filo pastry, defrosted if frozen

25 g (1 oz) butter, melted

25 g (1 oz) Parmesan cheese, freshly grated

salt and pepper

salad leaves dressed with olive oil and lemon juice, to serve

- Heat the oil in a large, heavy-based frying pan and cook the onion and garlic over a medium heat, stirring occasionally, for 5 minutes. Add the pine nuts and spinach and cook, stirring, for 3–4 minutes until heated through.

- Remove the pan from the heat and tip the mixture into a bowl. Add the whole eggs, egg yolks, feta and nutmeg, stir well and season with a little salt and plenty of pepper. Transfer to a large gratin dish.

- Crumple the sheets of filo pastry over the top, brush with the melted butter and scatter over the Parmesan. Place in a preheated oven, 180°C (350°F), Gas Mark 4, for 10–12 minutes until the pastry is golden and crisp.

- Serve hot with salad leaves dressed with olive oil and lemon juice.

---

 1 Spinach and Cheese Pesto Pasta

Bring a large saucepan of lightly salted water to the boil and cook 2 x 250 g (8 oz) packs fresh spinach and ricotta tortellini for 2–3 minutes until just tender. Drain the pasta, return to the pan and stir in 4 tablespoons green pesto. Serve in warmed bowls, scattered with Parmesan cheese shavings.

 2 Spinach and Cheese Baked Eggs

In a bowl, mix together 1 kg (2 lb) defrosted and well-drained frozen spinach, 2 x 200 g (7 oz) packs feta cheese, drained and crumbled, and 2 tablespoons Greek yogurt. Divide the mixture between 4 individual ramekins, then break an egg into each ramekin and season with salt and pepper. Top each ramekin with 1 tablespoon Greek yogurt. Place the ramekins in a baking tin and pour in enough boiling water to come halfway up the sides of the ramekins. Place on the centre shelf of a preheated oven, 180°C (350°F), Gas Mark 4, for 10 minutes. Serve immediately.

30 Vegetable, Fruit and Nut Biryani

Serves 4

250 g (8 oz) basmati rice
½ cauliflower, broken into florets
2 tablespoons vegetable oil
2 large sweet potatoes, peeled
  and cut into cubes
1 large onion, sliced
3 tablespoons hot curry paste
½ teaspoon ground turmeric
2 teaspoons mustard seeds
300 ml (½ pint) hot vegetable
  stock
250 g (8 oz) fine green beans,
  topped and tailed and halved
100 g (3½ oz) sultanas
6 tablespoons chopped coriander
50 g (2 oz) cashew nuts, lightly
  toasted

- Bring a large saucepan of lightly salted water to the boil and cook the rice for 5 minutes. Add the cauliflower and cook with the rice for a further 10 minutes or until both are tender, then drain.

- Meanwhile, heat the oil in a large, heavy-based frying pan and cook the sweet potatoes and onion over a medium heat, stirring occasionally, for 10 minutes until browned and tender. Add the curry paste, turmeric and mustard seeds and cook, stirring, for a further 2 minutes.

- Pour in the stock and add the green beans. Bring to the boil, then reduce the heat and simmer for 5 minutes.

- Stir in the drained rice and cauliflower, sultanas, coriander and cashew nuts and simmer for a further 2 minutes. Serve spooned on to warmed serving plates with poppadums and raita.

 1 Speedy Vegetable Biryani

Cook 250 g (8 oz) frozen cauliflower florets and 250 g (8 oz) frozen green beans in a large saucepan of lightly salted water according to the pack instructions. Drain and return to the pan, add a 400 g (13 oz) jar biryani curry sauce and heat through gently. Meanwhile, heat 400 g (13 oz) ready-cooked pilau rice according to the pack instructions. Serve the rice alongside the curry, scattered with lightly toasted cashew nuts, with poppadums and raita.

 2 Curried Vegetable Gratin

Melt 25 g (1 oz) butter in a large saucepan, add 25 g (1 oz) plain flour and cook over a medium heat, stirring, for a few seconds. Remove from the heat and add 300 ml (½ pint) milk, a little at a time, stirring well between each addition. Stir in 50 g (2 oz) grated Cheddar cheese and ½ teaspoon curry powder. Return to the heat, then bring to the boil, stirring constantly, cooking until thickened. Add 500 g (1 lb) mixed frozen vegetables, such as carrots, green beans and cauliflower florets, and toss with the sauce. Divide between individual gratin dishes, then sprinkle with 2 tablespoons fresh white breadcrumbs. Stand on a baking sheet and cook under a preheated high grill for 8–10 minutes until browned and the vegetables are piping hot.

Vegetable Pad Thai

Serves 4

175 g (6 oz) rice stick noodles
2 tablespoons sesame oil
2 eggs, beaten
1 tablespoon vegetable oil
200 g (7 oz) bean sprouts
1 bunch of spring onions, trimmed and roughly chopped
1 teaspoon dried chilli flakes
1 tablespoon Thai fish sauce
1 tablespoon soft light brown sugar
50 g (2 oz) salted peanuts, roughly chopped
4 tablespoons chopped fresh coriander
lime wedges, to serve

- Place the rice noodles in a large heatproof bowl, cover with boiling water and leave to soak for 10 minutes, or according to the packet instructions, until tender. Drain and toss with 1 tablespoon of the sesame oil.

- Meanwhile, heat the remaining sesame oil in a large, heavy-based frying pan, pour in the eggs in a thin layer and cook over a medium heat for 1–2 minutes until golden and set. Remove, shred and add to the noodles.

- Heat the vegetable oil in the pan and stir-fry the bean sprouts and spring onions over a high heat for 2–3 minutes until softened, then add the chilli flakes and stir well. Mix the fish sauce with the sugar and toss into the noodle mixture, then add to the pan with the peanuts and cook, tossing, for 2–4 minutes until piping hot.

- Serve in warmed serving bowls sprinkled with the coriander, with lime wedges for squeezing over.

 Instant Pad Thai Noodles

Beat 2 eggs in a bowl. Heat 1 tablespoon sesame oil in a large, heavy-based frying pan, pour in the eggs in a thin layer and cook over a medium heat for 1–2 minutes until golden and set. Remove, shred and add to 375 g (12 oz) ready-cooked rice noodles. Heat 1 tablespoon vegetable oil in the pan and stir-fry 200 g (7 oz) bean sprouts and 1 bunch of trimmed and shredded spring onions over a high heat for 2–3 minutes until softened. Add the noodles and shredded omelette and 120 g (4 oz) Pad Thai stir-fry sauce and toss until heated through. Scatter over some salted peanuts to serve.

Pad Thai-Style Sweet Potatoes and Sugar Snap Peas Heat 2 tablespoons vegetable oil in a large frying pan and cook 750 g (1½ lb) sweet potatoes, peeled and chopped, over a medium heat, stirring, for 8–10 minutes until soft. Add 250 g (8 oz) sugar snap peas, 1 bunch of chopped spring onions, 3 tablespoons soft light brown sugar, 2 tablespoons Thai fish sauce and 1 teaspoon dried chilli flakes and cook, stirring, for 6–8 minutes. Scatter over 50 g (2 oz) chopped coriander and 125 g (4 oz) toasted cashew nuts.

3 Chunky Vegetable Red Lentil Dahl

Serves 4

4 tablespoons vegetable oil
1 large onion, roughly chopped
1 aubergine, trimmed and roughly chopped
1 red pepper, cored, deseeded and cut into chunks
250 g (8 oz) okra, trimmed and cut into 2.5 cm (1 inch) lengths
175 g (6 oz) split red lentils, rinsed
3 tablespoons balti curry paste
600 ml (1 pint) vegetable stock
3 tablespoons chopped mint
200 g (7 oz) natural yogurt
5 tablespoons chopped fresh coriander
salt and pepper
warm naan breads, to serve

- Heat the oil in a large, heavy-based saucepan and cook the onion and aubergine over a medium heat, stirring occasionally, for 5 minutes, until softened and cooked through.

- Add the red pepper and okra to the pan and cook, stirring frequently, for 3–4 minutes before adding the lentils and curry paste. Stir well to mix, then pour in the stock. Bring to the boil, then reduce the heat, cover and simmer for 20 minutes until the lentils are tender.

- Meanwhile, stir the mint into the yogurt.

- Remove the pan from the heat, stir in the coriander and season with a little salt and pepper. Serve with the minted yogurt and warm naan breads.

 Quick Red Lentil, Chunky Vegetable and Chilli Soup Heat 2 tablespoons olive oil in a saucepan and cook 2 chopped onions, 1 finely chopped red chilli, the finely grated rind of 1 lemon and 1 teaspoon ground cumin over a medium heat, stirring, for 2 minutes. Add 200 g (7 oz) rinsed split red lentils, 200 g (7 oz) frozen chunky mixed vegetables and 750 ml (1¼ pints) hot vegetable stock, and simmer for 8 minutes until the lentils are tender. Stir through shredded mint and serve with natural yogurt and pitta breads.

 Chunky Vegetable Balti Heat 4 tablespoons vegetable oil in a large, heavy-based saucepan and cook 1 large roughly chopped onion and 1 trimmed and roughly chopped aubergine over a medium heat, stirring occasionally, for 5 minutes until softened and cooked through. Add 1 red pepper, cored, deseeded and cut into chunks, and 250 g (8 oz) trimmed okra, cut into 2.5 cm (1 inch) lengths, and cook, stirring frequently for 3–4 minutes. Stir in 3 tablespoons balti curry paste, then add 600 ml (1 pint) vegetable stock. Bring to the boil, then reduce the heat, cover and simmer for 10 minutes. Meanwhile, prepare the minted yogurt as above. Serve with ready-cooked pilau rice, heated through according to the pack instructions, and warm naan breads.

Rich Tomato and Chilli Spaghetti

Serves 4

250 g (8 oz) dried spaghetti
2 tablespoons olive oil
2 shallots, finely chopped
1 red chilli, finely chopped
2 garlic cloves, thinly sliced
500 g (1 lb) tomatoes, roughly
  chopped
3 tablespoons sun-dried tomato
  paste
150 ml (¼ pint) red wine
6 tablespoons chopped parsley
salt and pepper
freshly grated Parmesan cheese,
  to serve (optional)

- Bring a large saucepan of lightly salted water to the boil and cook the spaghetti for 8–10 minutes until just tender. Drain, return to the pan and toss with 1 tablespoon of the oil.

- Meanwhile, heat the remaining oil in a large, heavy-based frying pan and cook the shallots, chilli and garlic over a medium heat, stirring frequently, for 2–3 minutes until slightly softened. Add the tomatoes, increase the heat and cook, stirring occasionally, for 5 minutes until beginning to soften. Stir in the tomato paste and wine, cover and simmer for 10 minutes until thick and pulpy.

- Stir in the parsley and season with pepper. Add the cooked spaghetti and toss well to coat in the sauce. Serve with freshly grated Parmesan, if liked.

 Easy Tomato, Chilli and Black Olive Spaghetti Bring a large saucepan of salted water to the boil and cook the spaghetti for 8–10 minutes until just tender. Drain, return to the pan and toss with 1 tablespoon olive oil. Meanwhile, heat 2 tablespoons olive oil in a large frying pan and cook 2 finely chopped shallots, 1 finely chopped red chilli and 2 thinly sliced garlic cloves over a medium heat, stirring, for 2–3 minutes until softened. Add a 500 g (1 lb) jar red wine-flavoured ragu sauce and a drained 250 g (8 oz) jar pitted black olives, chopped, and heat through. Stir in 6 tablespoons chopped parsley, season with pepper and serve with freshly grated Parmesan cheese.

 Roasted Aubergine and Tomato Spaghetti Bring a large saucepan of lightly salted water to the boil and cook 250 g (8 oz) dried spaghetti for 8–10 minutes until just tender. Drain, return to the pan and toss with 1 tablespoon olive oil. Meanwhile, trim and chop 1 aubergine into large chunks. Toss with 4 tablespoons olive oil in a roasting tin and place in a preheated oven, 220°C (425°F), Gas Mark 7, for 20 minutes. While the pasta and aubergine are cooking, heat 2 tablespoons olive oil in a large, heavy-based frying pan and cook 2 finely chopped shallots, 1 finely chopped red chilli and 2 thinly sliced garlic cloves over a medium heat, stirring frequently, for 2–3 minutes until slightly softened. Add 500 g (1 lb) tomatoes, increase the heat and cook, stirring occasionally, for 5 minutes until beginning to soften. Stir in 3 tablespoons sun-dried tomato paste and 150 ml (¼ pint) red wine, cover and simmer for 10 minutes until thick and pulpy, adding the roasted aubergine towards the end of the cooking time. Stir in 6 tablespoons chopped parsley and season with pepper. Add the spaghetti and toss well. Serve immediately.

30 Cauliflower and Potato Curry with Spinach

Serves 4

3 tablespoons vegetable oil
1 large onion, roughly chopped
1 cauliflower, trimmed and cut into florets
500 g (1 lb) potatoes, peeled and cut into chunks
2 teaspoons cumin seeds
4 tablespoons korma curry paste
400 g (13 oz) can coconut milk
300 ml (½ pint) vegetable stock
300 g (10 oz) spinach leaves
4 tablespoons chopped fresh coriander
salt and pepper
warm naan breads, to serve

- Heat the oil in a large, heavy-based saucepan and cook the onion over a medium heat, stirring occasionally, for 2–3 minutes until beginning to soften, then add the cauliflower, potatoes and cumin seeds. Cook for 4–5 minutes, stirring occasionally, until the potatoes are beginning to brown.

- Add the curry paste and toss to coat the vegetables, then stir in the coconut milk and stock and bring to the boil. Reduce the heat, cover and simmer, stirring occasionally, for 20 minutes until the vegetables are tender, adding the spinach for the last 5 minutes of the cooking time.

- Season generously with salt and pepper and stir in the coriander. Serve with warm naan breads.

 Cauliflower Thai Green Curry

Cook a 500 g (1 lb) mixture of frozen cauliflower florets and green beans in a large saucepan of slightly salted boiling water according to the pack instructions. Drain and return to the pan. Add a 400 g (13 oz) jar Thai green curry sauce and heat through, stirring gently. Serve with ready-cooked Thai Jasmine rice, heated through according to the pack instructions.

 Baked Cauliflower and Spinach Gratin

Trim 1 cauliflower, reserving a few inner leaves, and cut into florets. Place in a steamer with 2 torn bay leaves tucked among the florets and a few fresh gratings of nutmeg. Steam for 12 minutes until the cauliflower is tender. Meanwhile, rinse 300 g (10 oz) spinach leaves, place in a large saucepan over a medium heat and stir gently until wilted. Squeeze out the excess moisture. Place the cauliflower and spinach in a large, greased gratin dish and pour over a 350 g (11½ oz) tub fresh cheese sauce. Sprinkle over 100 g (3½ oz) fresh white breadcrumbs and grate 50 g (2 oz) Parmesan cheese on top. Place in a preheated oven, 200°C (400°F), Gas Mark 6, for 8 minutes until golden and bubbling. Serve with a green salad.

30 Butternut Squash, Tomato and Red Onion Gratin

Serves 4

75 g (3 oz) butter
2 red onions, sliced
750 g (1½ lb) butternut
squash, peeled, deseeded
and thinly sliced
2 tablespoons chopped parsley
3 tomatoes, thinly sliced
150 ml (¼ pint) vegetable stock
25 g (1 oz) plain flour
300 ml (½ pint) milk
½ teaspoon freshly grated nutmeg
1 teaspoon Dijon mustard
150 g (5 oz) Emmental or Gruyère
cheese, grated

To serve

crusty bread
salad

- Melt 50 g (2 oz) of the butter in a large, heavy-based frying pan or wok and cook the onions and squash over a medium-high heat, stirring occasionally, for 5 minutes until beginning to soften and brown in places. Add the parsley, tomatoes and stock and bring to the boil. Reduce the heat, cover and simmer for 5 minutes.

- Meanwhile, melt the remaining 25 g (1 oz) butter in a saucepan, add the flour and cook over a medium heat, stirring, for a few seconds. Remove from the heat and add the milk, a little at a time, stirring well between each addition. Return to the heat, then bring to the boil, stirring constantly, cooking until thickened. Remove from the heat, add the nutmeg, mustard and half the cheese and stir well. Add to the pan with the squash and toss together.

- Transfer to a large gratin dish, sprinkle with the remaining cheese and cook under a preheated medium grill for 10 minutes until golden and bubbling. Serve with crusty bread and a simple salad.

---

1 Butternut, Sun-Dried Tomato and Red Onion Spaghetti
Cook 500 g (1 lb) fresh spaghetti in a saucepan of lightly salted boiling water for 3–4 minutes or until just tender, then drain. Meanwhile, heat 1 tablespoon olive oil in a large, heavy-based frying pan and cook 1 finely chopped red onion over a medium heat, stirring frequently, for 5 minutes until softened. While the onion is cooking, cook 300 g (10 oz) ready-prepared butternut squash in a microwave oven according to the pack instructions, then add to the onion. Stir in 8 sun-dried tomatoes, drained and chopped, and 3 tablespoons balsamic vinegar, then add the drained pasta. Season and toss together with 2 handfuls of chopped basil and 200 g (7 oz) feta cheese, drained and crumbled.

2 Butternut Squash, Tomato and Red Onion Pasta Melt 50 g (2 oz) butter in a large frying pan and cook 2 sliced red onions and 750 g (1½ lb) thinly-sliced butternut squash over a medium heat, stirring, for 5 minutes until soft and brown in places. Add 2 tablespoons chopped parsley, 3 sliced tomatoes and 150 ml (¼ pint) vegetable stock and bring to the boil. Cover and simmer for 5 minutes. Meanwhile, cook 250 g (8 oz) dried fusilli according to the pack instructions. Add to the sauce and toss together.

1 Coconut Dahl with Toasted Naan Fingers

Serves 4

1 tablespoon vegetable oil
1 onion, roughly chopped
2 tablespoons korma curry paste
125 g (4 oz) split red lentils, rinsed
400 g (13 oz) can coconut milk
naan breads, to serve

- Heat the oil in a heavy-based saucepan and cook the onion over a high heat, stirring, for 1 minute, then stir in the curry paste and lentils. Pour in the coconut milk, then fill the can with water and add to the lentils. Simmer briskly, uncovered, for 8–9 minutes until the lentils are tender and the mixture is thick and pulpy.

- Meanwhile, lightly toast the naan breads under a preheated high grill until warm and golden. Cut into fingers and serve alongside the dahl for dipping.

2 Coconut Dahl with Curried Onion

Naan Breads Make the dahl as above. Meanwhile, heat 2 tablespoons oil in a large, heavy-based frying pan and cook 2 chopped onions and 1 chopped red onion over a medium heat, stirring occasionally, for 5 minutes until softened. Add 8 tablespoons coconut milk, 3 tablespoons korma curry paste, 1 tablespoon mustard seeds and 200 g (7 oz) spinach leaves and cook, stirring, for 2 minutes until the spinach has wilted. Lightly toast 2 naan breads on one side under a preheated medium grill. Turn over, divide the onion mixture between the naan breads and scatter with 4 tablespoons chopped fresh coriander and 2 tablespoons desiccated coconut. Lightly toast for 3–4 minutes until the coconut is golden. Serve each warm naan cut in half alongside the dahl.

3 Chunky Vegetable Dahl with Toasted

Naan Fingers Heat 4 tablespoons vegetable oil in a large saucepan and cook 1 roughly chopped onion, 1 trimmed and roughly chopped large courgette and 1 trimmed and roughly chopped aubergine over a medium-high heat, stirring occasionally, for 10 minutes until tender. Stir in 4 tablespoons korma curry paste and 125 g (4 oz) rinsed split red lentils, then pour in 600 ml (1 pint) vegetable stock and simmer for 10–15 minutes until thick and pulpy. Meanwhile, prepare the toasted naan fingers as above and serve with the dahl.

30 Puy Lentil Stew with Garlic and Herb Bread

Serves 4

4 tablespoons olive oil
1 red pepper, cut into chunks
1 green pepper, cut into chunks
1 red onion, roughly chopped
1 garlic clove, sliced
1 fennel bulb, trimmed and sliced
250 g (8 oz) Puy lentils, rinsed
600 ml (1 pint) vegetable stock
300 ml (½ pint) red wine

For the garlic bread

50 g (2 oz) butter, softened
1 garlic clove, crushed
2 tablespoons thyme leaves,
   roughly chopped
1 wholemeal French baguette
salt and pepper

- Heat the oil in a large, heavy-based saucepan and cook the peppers, onion, garlic and fennel over a medium-high heat, stirring frequently, for 5 minutes until softened and lightly browned. Stir in the lentils, stock and wine and bring to the boil, then reduce the heat and simmer for 25 minutes until the lentils are tender.

- Meanwhile, beat the softened butter with the garlic and thyme in a bowl and season with a little salt and pepper. Cut the baguette into thick slices, almost all the way through but leaving the base attached. Spread the butter thickly over each slice, then wrap the baguette in foil and place in a preheated oven, 200°C (400°F), Gas Mark 6, for 15 minutes.

- Serve the stew hot, ladled into warm serving bowls, with the torn hot garlic and herb bread on the side for mopping up the juices.

10 Chunky Tomato and Puy Lentil Soup

Heat 1 tablespoon olive oil in a large saucepan and cook 1 finely chopped onion over a medium-high heat, stirring frequently, for 5 minutes. Add a 400 g (13 oz) can chopped tomatoes, a drained 400 g (13 oz) can Puy lentils and 1 crushed garlic clove. Bring to the boil, then simmer for 4 minutes until warmed through. Season with salt and pepper. Divide between 4 warmed soup bowls and garnish each serving with 1 tablespoon soured cream and torn basil leaves. Serve with warm crusty bread.

20 Puy Lentil and Sun-Dried

Tomato Salad Place 200 g (7 oz) rinsed Puy lentils in a saucepan, cover generously with cold water and bring to the boil. Reduce the heat and simmer for 15 minutes until just tender. Drain, then toss with the juice of 1 lemon, 1 crushed garlic clove and 4 tablespoons olive oil, and season with salt and pepper. Stir a drained 280 g (9¼ oz) jar sun-dried tomatoes, 1 small finely chopped red onion and a handful of chopped flat leaf parsley through the lentils and serve with some rocket leaves.

QuickCook
Fuss-Free Family Desserts

Recipes listed by cooking time

Gingered Apricots with Mascarpone and Brioche

Serves 4

25 g (1 oz) butter

375 g (12 oz) apricots, stoned and quartered

50 g (2 oz) soft light brown sugar

6 tablespoons stem ginger syrup

2 pieces of stem ginger, finely chopped

250 g (8 oz) tub mascarpone cheese

2 tablespoons demerara sugar

toasted slices of brioche, to serve

- Melt the butter in a heavy-based frying pan and cook the apricots over a medium heat, stirring occasionally, for 3–4 minutes until soft and browned in places. Sprinkle over the brown sugar and cook, stirring, for 1 minute. Add the stem ginger syrup, stir well and cook for a further 1 minute, then remove from the heat.

- Mix the stem ginger with the mascarpone and demerara sugar.

- Serve the apricots on warm toasted brioche with a spoonful of the ginger cream on top, allowing it to melt.

 Quick Gingered Apricots with Amaretti Melt 25 g (1 oz) butter in a heavy-based saucepan and cook a well-drained 400 g (13 oz) can halved apricots over a high heat, stirring, for 2–3 minutes. Sprinkle over 50 g (2 oz) soft light brown sugar and cook for 2–3 minutes, allowing the sugar to caramelize slightly. Pour over 2 tablespoons orange juice and heat for 1 minute, then transfer to a warmed serving dish and scatter over 8 lightly crushed amaretti biscuits. Serve with Greek yogurt.

 Gingered Nectarines and Peaches Heat 100 g (3½ oz) caster sugar, a 3.5 cm (1½ inch) piece of fresh root ginger, peeled and grated, and 400 ml (14 fl oz) pomegranate juice in a heavy-based saucepan for 2 minutes until the sugar has dissolved. Bring to the boil, then simmer for 10 minutes until reduced to a syrup. Stone 4 nectarines and 4 peaches. Cut each nectarine into 8 wedges and each peach into quarters. Add to the hot syrup and leave to cool slightly, then add 175 g (6 oz) fresh raspberries. Stir through 2 pieces of chopped stem ginger and serve with Greek yogurt.

30 Chocolate and Raspberry Layers

Serves 4

200 g (7 oz) bar plain dark
  chocolate, broken into pieces
300 ml (½ pint) double cream
250 g (8 oz) fresh raspberries
cocoa powder, for dusting
mint sprigs, to decorate
  (optional)

- Place the chocolate in a heatproof bowl and set over a saucepan of gently simmering water. Stir until melted and smooth, then remove from the heat. Line 2 baking sheets with baking parchment and spoon 12 x 10 cm (4 inch) rounds of melted chocolate on to the paper. Refrigerate or freeze for 15 minutes until firm and set.

- Meanwhile, whip the cream in a bowl until soft peaks form. Place the raspberries in a bowl and very lightly mash with a fork until lightly crushed and juicy. Fold the crushed raspberries into the whipped cream.

- Carefully peel the discs of chocolate away from the paper. Place a chocolate disc on each of 4 chilled dessert plates, top with half the raspberry cream and add another chocolate disc to each stack. Top with the remaining raspberry cream and chocolate discs. Dust a little cocoa powder over each stack and decorate with a mint sprig, if liked.

1 Speedy and Naughty Raspberry Ice Cream Sundae Place a 200 g (7 oz) bar white chocolate, broken into pieces, in a heatproof bowl and set over a saucepan of gently simmering water. Stir until melted and smooth, then remove from the heat. Meanwhile, in each of 4 serving glasses place 1 scoop vanilla ice cream, followed by 1 scoop raspberry ice cream and then another scoop of vanilla ice cream. Scatter over some fresh raspberries and pour over the melted white chocolate. Serve immediately.

2 Raspberry Fool Place 250 g (8 oz) fresh raspberries in a frying pan and lightly crush with a fork. Add 150 g (5 oz) caster sugar and 2 teaspoons lemon juice and cook over a medium-low heat, stirring gently, until the sugar has dissolved. Simmer for 3 minutes until the raspberries are soft and the juices are syrupy, then leave to cool. Whip 300 ml (½ pint) double cream in a bowl until soft peaks form. Fold through the raspberry mixture with 125 g (4 oz) whole fresh raspberries. Spoon into serving glasses.

Make-Ahead Cheesecakes with Berry Compote

Serves 4

8 gingernut biscuits
25 g (1 oz) butter, melted
400 g (13 oz) soft cheese
75 g (3 oz) caster sugar
finely grated rind and juice
   of 1 lime
3 tablespoons single cream
75 g (3 oz) fresh raspberries
75 g (3 oz) fresh blueberries
2 tablespoons grenadine

- Place the biscuits in a polythene bag and bash with a rolling pin to form fine crumbs. Tip into a saucepan or jug with the melted butter and mix well. Divide between 4 individual ramekins and press to form a firm base. Refrigerate while making the topping.

- Beat together the soft cheese, sugar and lime rind and juice in a bowl until smooth. Fold in the cream, then spoon over the cheesecake bases and roughly spread. Refrigerate for 5–10 minutes while making the compote.

- In a separate bowl, gently mix the berries with the grenadine.

- Serve the cheesecakes with the berry compote spooned on top in the centre.

Mini Berry Cheesecake Tartlets Beat 4 tablespoons lemon curd into 400 g (13 oz) soft cheese. Pour 1 teaspoon summer fruit sauce from a 200 g (7 oz) jar into each of 8 shop-bought ready-made sweet dessert tartlet cases. Top with a spoonful of the cheese mixture and then scatter over 200 g (7 oz) mixed fresh berries. Serve with a sifting of icing sugar.

Raspberry Cheesecake with Raspberry Liqueur Place 150 g (5 oz) digestive biscuits in a polythene bag and bash with a rolling pin to form fine crumbs. Mix with 25 g (1 oz) toasted flaked almonds and 75 g (3 oz) melted butter in a bowl. Press into a 20 cm (8 inch) loose-bottomed tart tin and refrigerate. Beat together 400 g (13 oz) soft cheese, 75 g (3 oz) caster sugar and the rind and juice of 1 lemon. Fold in 150 ml (¼ pint) double cream, then spread over the biscuit base and refrigerate until ready to serve. Make a raspberry compote by warming 300 g (10 oz) fresh raspberries with 2 tablespoons icing sugar in a saucepan. Crush lightly with a fork. Add 2–3 tablespoons crème de framboise liqueur and stir. Spoon on top of the cheesecake before serving.

Pear and Chocolate Crumble

Serves 4

3 x 410 g (13½ oz) cans pears, drained

5 tablespoons dark muscovado sugar

250 g (8 oz) plain flour

100 g (3½ oz) butter at room temperature, cut into cubes

100 g (3½ oz) demerara sugar

100 g (3½ oz) milk chocolate, very roughly chopped

1 tablespoon custard powder

2 tablespoons cocoa powder

1 tablespoon caster sugar

300 ml (½ pint) milk

- Roughly chop the pears and place in a bowl, add the muscovado sugar and toss well to coat. Transfer to a large gratin dish.

- Place the flour and butter in a food processor and pulse until coarse breadcrumbs form. Transfer to a bowl and stir in the demerara sugar and chocolate.

- Scatter the crumble mixture over the top of the pears and place in a preheated oven, 220°C (425°F), Gas Mark 7, for 10–12 minutes until just beginning to brown.

- Meanwhile, place the custard powder, cocoa and caster sugar in a heatproof bowl and blend to a paste with about 1 tablespoon of the milk. Heat the remaining milk in a saucepan until almost boiling, then pour on to the custard powder mixture, stirring constantly. Return the mixture to the pan and bring to the boil over a gentle heat, stirring constantly, until thickened.

- Serve the crumble hot with the chocolate custard.

Pan-Fried Pears with Chocolate Sauce Drain 3 x 410 g (13½ oz) cans pears and cut each in half. Melt 25 g (1 oz) unsalted butter in a large saucepan and cook the pears over a high heat, stirring frequently, for 2 minutes. Stir in 1 tablespoon soft light brown sugar and cook for a further minute. Add 75 g (3 oz) roughly chopped plain dark chocolate and 2 tablespoons double cream. Reduce the heat to low and stir constantly until the chocolate has melted and the sauce becomes glossy and smooth. Serve warm.

Chewy Chocolate and Pear Cookies Place 250 g (8 oz) plain flour and 100 g (3½ oz) butter at room temperature, cut into cubes, in a food processor and pulse until coarse breadcrumbs form. Add 1 egg and process briefly to mix, then add 100 g (3½ oz) very roughly chopped milk chocolate and 1 peeled, cored and chopped small pear and process again briefly. Form into 15 balls, then press on to a lightly greased baking sheet, using a fork to flatten them a little. Bake a preheated oven, 220°C (425°F), Gas Mark 7, for 12 minutes until just beginning to brown. Serve slightly warm.

 Raspberry Rice Brûlée

Serves 4

75 g (3 oz) fresh raspberries
1 tablespoon caster sugar
1 tablespoon water
425 g (14 oz) can rice pudding
4 tablespoons double cream
125 g (4 oz) light muscovado
   sugar

- Place the raspberries in a saucepan with the caster sugar and measurement water and heat gently for 2 minutes until the raspberries are slightly softenened. Divide between 4 individual ramekins.

- Gently heat the rice pudding and cream in a separate saucepan for 2 minutes until hot. Spoon the rice mixture over the raspberries, then top with a thick layer of the muscovado sugar and level.

- Stand the ramekins on a baking sheet and cook under a preheated high grill for 1–2 minutes until the sugar caramelizes and becomes crisp. Serve warm.

 Traditional Crème Brûlée with Raspberries Place 75 g (3 oz) fresh raspberries in a saucepan with 1 tablespoon each caster sugar and water, and heat gently for 2 minutes until the raspberries are slightly softened. Divide between 4 individual ramekins. Bring 300 ml (½ pint) milk to the boil. Meanwhile, beat together 2 egg yolks, 4 tablespoons each caster sugar and double cream and 1 tablespoon cornflour in a heatproof bowl. Pour over the hot milk, stirring constantly, then return the mixture to the rinsed-out pan and gently heat, stirring constantly, until a thick custard is formed. Pour over the raspberries in the ramekins. Scatter over 125 g (4 oz) light muscovado sugar. Using a kitchen blowtorch, cook the sugar until it has caramelized. Serve warm.

Vanilla Rice Pudding with Raspberry Compote Place 250 g (8 oz) Arborio risotto rice in a saucepan with 600 ml (1 pint) milk, 300 ml (½ pint) double cream and 1 vanilla pod, split lengthways. Bring to the boil and add 125 g (4 oz) soft light brown sugar. Reduce the heat, cover and simmer for 20–25 minutes until the rice is tender. Meanwhile, place 175 g (6 oz) raspberries in a saucepan with 50 g (2 oz) caster sugar and 1 tablespoon water. Heat gently, stirring occasionally, for 2–3 minutes until the sugar dissolves and the fruit is soft and warm. Remove the vanilla pod from the rice and serve the rice pudding in warmed serving bowls, with the compote spooned on top.

White Chocolate Cream with Raspberries

Serves 4

150 g (5 oz) white chocolate, broken into pieces, plus extra shavings to decorate
300 ml (½ pint) double cream
200 ml (7 fl oz) crème fraîche
125 g (4 oz) fresh raspberries, lightly mashed
plain dark chocolate shavings, to decorate

- Place the white chocolate in a saucepan with 8 tablespoons of the cream and gently heat, stirring constantly, until the chocolate has melted and the mixture is smooth. Remove from the heat.

- Place the remaining cream in a plastic bowl and whisk until soft peaks form. Fold in the crème fraîche, then fold in the warm chocolate mixture. Finally, fold in the raspberries. Freeze in the bowl for 5 minutes.

- Divide the mixture between 4 serving glasses and decorate with white and plain dark chocolate shavings.

 Chunky Chocolate Cream with Raspberries Whip 300 ml (½ pint) double cream until soft peaks form. Roughly chop 160 g (5½ oz) white chocolate and scatter over the whipped cream. Lightly crush 100 g (3½ oz) fresh raspberries with a fork on a plate, then fold into the cream with the chocolate until marbled. Spoon into 4 serving glasses.

 Rum Cream with Strawberries In a food processor, whizz 400 g (13 oz) hulled strawberries (reserving a few for decoration) with 50 g (2 oz) caster sugar until puréed, then refrigerate. Whip 150 ml (¼ pint) double cream in a bowl until slightly thickened, then fold in 25 g (1 oz) caster sugar, 1 tablespoon dark rum and ½ teaspoon vanilla extract. In each of 4 serving glasses make alternate layers of the strawberry purée and cream mixture, finishing with the cream. Refrigerate until ready to serve. Decorate with the reserved strawberries and serve with shop-bought shortbread fingers, if liked.

3⃝ Warm Spiced Plums with Ice Cream

Serves 4

750 g (1½ lb) ripe plums, halved
  and stoned
100 g (3½ oz) caster sugar
½ teaspoon ground cinnamon
½ teaspoon ground ginger
3 tablespoons water
good-quality ice cream, to serve

- Place all the ingredients except the ice cream in a large, heavy-based saucepan and bring to the boil, stirring occasionally. Reduce the heat to low, cover and very gently simmer, stirring occasionally, for 15–20 minutes until the plums are tender.

- Transfer to a large serving dish and leave to cool for 5 minutes before serving.

- Serve with scoops of good-quality ice cream.

 Caramelized Plums, Apricots and Peaches Halve and stone a 750 g (1½ lb) mixture of ripe plums, apricots and peaches. Heat a large, nonstick frying pan over a medium heat. Press the cut side of each fruit half into a plate of sugar (any variety) and cook, sugar-side down, for 3–5 minutes or until the sugar has melted and turned golden. Leave to cool slightly, then serve with thick Greek yogurt drizzled with clear honey.

 Plums with Honey and Mascarpone Stone and slice 2 plums and 2 apricots and place in a serving bowl. Peel and slice 1 kiwifruit and stone and slice 250 g (8 oz) cherries. Add to the bowl with the plums and apricots and gently mix together. Mix 250 g (8 oz) mascarpone cheese with 2 tablespoons clear honey, ½ teaspoon vanilla extract and the seeds from 1 vanilla pod in a separate bowl. Spoon the fruit into dishes and serve the mascarpone mixture on the side.

30 Apricots with Lemon Cream and Soft Amaretti

Serves 4

500 g (1 lb) apricots, halved and
stoned
4 tablespoons soft light brown
sugar
1 vanilla pod, split lengthways
5 tablespoons water
finely grated rind of 1 lemon
200 ml (7 fl oz) crème fraîche

For the amaretti

1 egg white
75 g (3 oz) ground almonds
50 g (2 oz) caster sugar

- Place the apricots in a heavy-based saucepan with the brown sugar, vanilla pod and measurement water and bring to the boil. Reduce the heat, cover and simmer for 15 minutes until the apricots are tender yet just retaining their shape.

- Meanwhile, for the amaretti, whisk the egg white in a grease-free bowl until stiff. Fold in the ground almonds and caster sugar until well mixed. Line a baking sheet with baking parchment and spoon tablespoonfuls of the mixture on to the lined sheet, well spaced apart.

- Bake in a preheated oven, 190°C (375°F), Gas Mark 5, for 10 minutes until just beginning to brown. Leave to cool on the paper for 5 minutes, then carefully peel away from the paper and transfer to a wire rack.

- Mix the lemon rind into the crème fraîche. Remove the vanilla pod from the apricots and spoon the apricots into serving dishes. Serve with the lemon cream and soft amaretti.

 Apricot and Peach Pavlovas

Spoon 2 tablespoons extra-thick double cream into each of 4 shop-bought ready-made meringue nests. Drain 400 g (13 oz) canned apricots, thinly slice and arrange on top of the cream. Garnish each pavlova with a mint sprig.

 Apricot and Hot Cross Bun Pudding

Cut 4 shop-bought hot cross buns into chunks and place them in a greased ovenproof dish. Spoon 6 tablespoons apricot jam over the hot cross buns and pour 425 g (14 oz) ready-to-serve custard over the top. Place in a preheated oven, 180°C (350°F), Gas Mark 4, for 10–15 minutes until bubbling hot. Serve immediately.

FAM-DESS-COG

10 Eggy Fruit Bread with Berries and Cream

Serves 4

2 eggs
4 tablespoons milk
25 g (1 oz) caster sugar
½ teaspoon ground cinnamon
25 g (1 oz) butter
4 thick slices of fruit bread
125 g (4 oz) mixed fresh berries
8 tablespoons crème fraîche
icing sugar, for dusting
maple syrup, for drizzling

· Beat the eggs with the milk, caster sugar and cinnamon in a bowl. Melt the butter in a large, heavy-based frying pan. Dip the fruit bread slices, 2 at a time, into the egg mixture on both sides and allow to soak in the mixture, then lift out and cook over a medium heat for 1–2 minutes on each side until golden and set. Remove and stack to keep warm.

· Meanwhile, mix half the berries into the crème fraîche.

· Spoon the berry cream on to the warm toasts, then scatter over the remaining berries and dust with icing sugar. Drizzle with maple syrup and serve.

---

20 Eggy Chocolate Bread with Raspberries

Beat 2 eggs with 4 tablespoons good-quality shop-bought chocolate milkshake, 25 g (1 oz) caster sugar and ½ teaspoon ground cinnamon in a bowl. Melt 25 g (1 oz) butter in a large, heavy-based frying pan. Dip 4 thick slices of brioche, 2 at a time, into the egg mixture on both sides and allow to soak in the mixture, then lift out and cook over a medium heat for 1–2 minutes on each side until golden and set. Remove and stack to keep warm. Place 125 g (4 oz) chopped plain dark chocolate in a saucepan with 6 tablespoons double cream and 15 g (½ oz) butter. Heat gently, stirring constantly, until the sauce is smooth and melted. Serve the chocolate breads topped with spoonfuls of extra-thick double cream, scattered with 75 g (3 oz) fresh raspberries and 50 g (2 oz) roughly chopped plain dark chocolate, then drizzled with the warm chocolate sauce.

30 Berry Bread and Butter Pudding

Lightly butter 8 slices of fruit bread and layer in a large, shallow gratin dish with 125 g (4 oz) mixed berries, defrosted if frozen. Beat together 3 eggs, 450 ml (¾ pint) milk, 50 g (2 oz) caster sugar and ½ teaspoon ground cinnamon in a bowl, then pour over the bread and berries. Place in a preheated oven, 200°C (400°F), Gas Mark 6, for 20 minutes until lightly set and golden. Scatter with 2 tablespoons demerara sugar to serve.

30 Chocolate Mousse with Pistachio Ice Cream

Serves 6

200 g (7 oz) bar plain dark
  chocolate, broken into pieces
200 g (7 oz) unsalted butter, cut
  into cubes
3 eggs
75 g (3 oz) caster sugar
icing sugar, for dusting
pistachio or vanilla ice cream, to
  serve

- Place the chocolate and butter in a heatproof bowl and set over a saucepan of gently simmering water. Stir until melted and smooth, then remove from the heat.

- Whisk the eggs and sugar together in a large bowl until pale and thick, then fold in the melted chocolate and butter until well mixed.

- Divide between 6 individual ramekins and place on a baking sheet. Bake in a preheated oven, 150°C (300°C), Gas Mark 2, for 7 minutes until just firm.

- Leave to cool for 10 minutes, then dust with icing sugar and serve with a scoop of pistachio or vanilla ice cream on top of each mousse.

 Coffee-Drowned Ice Cream with Chocolate Liqueur Place small scoops of vanilla ice cream in the bottom of 6 small glasses. Pour over a little chilled chocolate liqueur and top with a shot of freshly made espresso coffee. Serve immediately.

 Bananas and Ice Cream with Rich Chocolate Sauce Place 50 g (2 oz) each butter, cocoa powder, soft light brown sugar and caster sugar in a saucepan. Add 200 ml (7 fl oz) milk and ½ teaspoon vanilla extract. Heat gently over a medium heat, stirring constantly, until a smooth consistency. Bring to the boil, then simmer until the sauce has thickened. Slice 1 banana into each of 6 serving glasses, add scoops of vanilla ice cream to each and pour over the sauce.

Banoffee Layers

Serves 4

6 digestive biscuits
2 large bananas
50 g (2 oz) butter
50 g (2 oz) soft dark brown sugar
150 ml (¼ pint) double cream
200 ml (7 fl oz) crème fraîche
grated plain dark chocolate,
   to decorate

- Place the biscuits in a polythene bag and bash with a rolling pin to form fine crumbs. Divide between 4 tall serving glasses and use to line each base.

- Mash one of the bananas and divide between the 4 glasses, spooning on top of the biscuit crumbs.

- Melt the butter in a small saucepan, add the sugar and heat over a medium heat, stirring well, until the sugar has dissolved. Add the cream and cook gently for 1–2 minutes until the mixture is thick. Remove from the heat and leave to cool for 1 minute, then spoon on top of the mashed banana.

- Slice the second banana and arrange on top of the caramel, then spoon over the crème fraîche. Decorate with grated plain dark chocolate before serving.

 Banoffee and Date Pudding

Lightly whip 300 ml (½ pint) double cream in a large bowl. Crumble in 4 shop-bought ready-made meringue nests, then fold in 4 sliced bananas and a handful of chopped pitted dates. Swirl over 4 tablespoons shop-bought toffee sauce. Spoon into 4 serving dishes, scatter with a handful of pecan nuts and drizzle with a little more toffee sauce.

 Quick-Fix Banoffee Pie

Line a 20 cm (8 inch) tart tin with clingfilm. In a food processor, whizz together 175 g (6 oz) pitted dates and 225 g (7½ oz) whole blanched almonds. Press into the tart tin and freeze for 10 minutes. Place 300 g (10 oz) Greek yogurt in a wide, shallow dish and sprinkle over 2 tablespoons dark muscovado sugar, then refrigerate for 5 minutes. Transfer to a serving plate, peeling away the clingfilm. Scatter over 2 sliced bananas. Swirl the sugar into the yogurt and spoon over, retaining the ripple effect. Finish with a grating of plain dark chocolate and serve immediately.

30 Oat-Topped Orchard Fruit Crumbles

Serves 4

4 cooking apples, peeled, cored and roughly chopped
2 tablespoons soft light brown sugar
2 tablespoons caster sugar
3 tablespoons water
175 g (6 oz) blackberries
100 g (3½ oz) plain flour
75 g (3 oz) unsalted butter, cut into cubes
100 g (3½ oz) porridge oats
100 g (3½ oz) demerara sugar
½ teaspoon ground cinnamon
ice cream, clotted cream or crème fraîche, to serve

- Place the apples, brown sugar, caster sugar and measurement water in a heavy-based saucepan and cook over a gentle heat, stirring occasionally, for 5–8 minutes until the apples are soft and just beginning to turn pulpy. Fold in the blackberries, cover and remove from the heat. Keep warm.

- Place the flour in a large bowl, add the butter and rub in with the fingertips until the mixture resembles coarse breadcrumbs. Stir in the oats, demerara sugar and cinnamon. Spread out in a large roasting tin and place in a preheated oven, 200°C (400°F), Gas Mark 6, for 10–15 minutes, stirring halfway through cooking, until golden.

- Spoon the warm fruit into warmed serving bowls and top with the warm golden crumble. Serve with ice cream, clotted cream or crème fraîche.

---

1 Quick Orchard Fruit Compote

Pudding Drain a 400 g (13 oz) can or jar apples or pears and roughly chop. Place in a saucepan with 3 tablespoons soft light brown sugar and cook over a medium heat, stirring occasionally, for 3–4 minutes. Divide 300 g (½ pint) Greek yogurt between 4 glass bowls. Swirl through the warm fruit compote and serve with shop-bought shortbread.

2 Mixed Summer Fruit Crumbles

Divide 200 g (7 oz) frozen mixed summer fruits between 4 ramekins. Sprinkle 2 teaspoons vanilla sugar and 1 teaspoon cornflour over each ramekin and stir around a little. Cover each with 1–2 tablespoons shop-bought ready-made crumble mix. Stand the ramekins on a baking sheet and place in a preheated oven, 220°C (425°F), Gas Mark 7, for 15 minutes. Serve with vanilla ice cream.

Pan-Fried Pineapple with Rum and Raisins

Serves 4

½ pineapple, skinned, cored and cut into thin slices

25 g (1 oz) unsalted butter

2 tablespoons soft dark brown sugar

4 tablespoons dark rum

4 tablespoons raisins

ice cream, to serve

- Halve each of the pineapple slices. Melt the butter in a large, heavy-based frying pan and cook the pineapple slices over a high heat for 2–3 minutes on each side until golden and softened. Sprinkle over the sugar, toss and cook for 1 minute, then pour in the rum and sprinkle over the raisins. Cook, tossing, for a further 2 minutes until heated through.

- Divide between 4 serving bowls and add a large scoop of vanilla ice cream to each serving.

Easy Pineapple, Mango and Passion Fruit Pan-Fry Melt 25 g (1 oz) butter in a large frying pan and cook 2 x 200 g (7 oz) packs prepared mixed fresh pineapple, mango and passion fruit over a high heat, turning frequently, for 3–4 minutes. Sprinkle over 2 tablespoons soft light brown sugar and 1 teaspoon mixed spice. Cook, tossing, for a further 2 minutes. Serve immediately with pouring cream.

Pineapple Flambé Skin and slice 1 pineapple, then remove the cores with an apple corer. Melt 50 g (2 oz) butter in a large frying pan and cook the pineapple slices in a single layer in batches for 90 seconds on each side. Transfer to a bowl. Add the seeds from 1 vanilla pod, 50 g (2 oz) light muscovado sugar and the juice of 1 orange to the pan and cook, stirring, until the sugar has dissolved.

Return the cooked pineapple and any juices to the pan and cook until piping hot. Pour over 3 tablespoons dark rum and set alight. Remove from the heat and allow the flames to die down, then serve with pouring cream.

30 Rhubarb and Ginger Tartlets

Serves 4

½ x 375 g (12 oz) pack sweet
  shortcrust pastry, defrosted if
  frozen
plain flour, for dusting
500 g (1 lb) rhubarb, trimmed and
  cut into chunks
50 g (2 oz) caster sugar
3 pieces of stem ginger, chopped
pinch of ground ginger
2 tablespoons stem ginger syrup
15 g (½ oz) unsalted butter
ice cream or crème fraîche, to
  serve

- Roll out the pastry on a lightly floured work surface and use to line 4 x 10 cm (4 inch) fluted tartlet tins. Prick the base of each a few times with a fork.

- Line each tartlet case with a piece of scrunched baking parchment and fill with baking beans. Place in a preheated oven, 200°C (400°F), Gas Mark 6, for 15 minutes, then remove the paper and beans and bake for a further 2–3 minutes.

- Meanwhile, place the rhubarb in a heavy-based saucepan with all the remaining ingredients except the ice cream or crème fraîche and cook over a medium heat, stirring occasionally, for 5 minutes. Reduce the heat and simmer gently, stirring occasionally, for 10 minutes until the rhubarb is tender and pulpy.

- Remove the tartlet cases from their tins. Place each on a serving plate and fill with the rhubarb mixture. Serve warm with ice cream or crème fraîche.

---

1 **Rhubarb and Ginger Compote** Cut 500 g (1 lb) trimmed rhubarb into 5 mm (¼ inch) slices. Place in a saucepan with 150 g (5 oz) caster sugar, 3 pieces of finely chopped stem ginger and 2 teaspoons vanilla extract and bring to the boil, stirring to help dissolve the sugar. Partially cover and simmer for about 3 minutes, then uncover and cook for a further 2 minutes until the rhubarb is tender. Pour into a jug and leave to cool a little until you are ready to serve with either vanilla ice cream or custard.

2 **Rhubarb and Ginger Trifle** Place 6 trimmed and roughly chopped rhubarb sticks in a saucepan with 100 ml (3½ fl oz) water and 150 g (5 oz) caster sugar and cook over a medium heat, stirring frequently, for 5 minutes. Strain, reserving the liquid, and leave to cool for 5 minutes. Stir 2 tablespoons Grand Marnier into the rhubarb liquid. Whip together 250 g (8 oz) mascarpone cheese, 125 g (4 oz) Greek yogurt and 50 g (2 oz) icing sugar in a bowl until thickened. Slice ½ shop-bought Jamaican ginger cake into 8 pieces. Place a slice of cake in the bottom of each of 4 wine glasses, then drizzle each with enough rhubarb liquid to moisten the sponge. Add a spoonful of rhubarb to each glass, top with another slice of cake and drizzle each with a little more rhubarb liquid. Top with the remaining rhubarb. Divide the mascarpone mixture between the glasses and sprinkle with toasted flaked almonds and chopped stem ginger.

FAM-DESS-CAO

30 Warm Creamy Coconut Rice with Mango and Lime

Serves 4

125 g (4 oz) Arborio risotto rice
75 g (3 oz) caster sugar
300 ml (½ pint) milk
400 g (13 oz) can coconut milk
½ mango, stoned, peeled and
   cut into small chunks
finely grated rind and juice of
   1 lime

- Place the rice in a heavy-based saucepan with the sugar, milk and coconut milk. Bring to the boil, then reduce the heat and simmer for 20 minutes until the rice has swelled and thickened.

- Meanwhile, place the mango in a bowl and mix with the lime rind and juice.

- Spoon the cooked rice into serving bowls and place spoonfuls of the mango and lime mixture into the centre of each.

1 Mango and Coconut Rice Pudding

Heat through 2 x 400 g (13 oz) cans rice pudding with ½ mango, stoned, peeled and roughly chopped, and 3 tablespoons lightly toasted desiccated coconut. Serve in large ramekins sprinkled with extra toasted desiccated coconut.

2 Coconut Rice with Caramelized

Banana Place 125 g (4 oz) Arborio risotto rice in a heavy-based saucepan with 75 g (3 oz) caster sugar, 300 ml (½ pint) milk and a 400 g (13 oz) can coconut milk. Bring to the boil, then reduce the heat and simmer for 20 minutes until the rice has swelled and thickened. Meanwhile, cut 4 firm bananas in half lengthways and sprinkle with 4 tablespoons soft light brown sugar and 1 teaspoon ground cinnamon. Heat a nonstick frying pan over a high heat and cook the bananas for 2 minutes on each side or until the sugar has caramelized. Spoon the cooked rice on to serving plates and top with the banana slices.

Griddled Madeira Cake with Plum and Berry Compote

Serves 4

25 g (1 oz) unsalted butter

2 plums, stoned and cut into chunks

175 g (6 oz) fresh strawberries, hulled and halved

50 g (2 oz) caster sugar

½ teaspoon ground cinnamon

2 tablespoons water

125 g (4 oz) fresh raspberries

4 thick slices of Madeira cake

2 tablespoons icing sugar

- Melt the butter in a heavy-based saucepan and cook the plums over a medium heat, stirring occasionally, for 2 minutes. Add the strawberries, caster sugar, cinnamon and measurement water and cook, stirring occasionally, for 2 minutes until the fruit is tender. Stir in the raspberries.

- Meanwhile, heat a griddle pan over a high heat. Dredge the cake slices on one side with half the icing sugar and cook, icing sugar-side down, for 1 minute until warm and scorched in lines, then dredge the other side with the remaining icing sugar and cook on that side for 1 minute.

- Serve the cake slices with the warm compote spooned over.

 Plum, Berry and Madeira Cake Trifles Melt 25 g (1 oz) butter in a heavy-based saucepan and cook 2 plums, stoned and cut into chunks, over a medium heat, stirring occasionally, for 2 minutes. Add 175 g (6 oz) hulled and halved strawberries, 50 g (2 oz) caster sugar, ½ teaspoon ground cinnamon and 1 tablespoon water and cook, stirring occasionally, for a further 2 minutes until the plums are tender. Leave to cool for 5 minutes, then spoon the compote into the base of a glass bowl and top with 4 slices of Madeira cake, cut into chunks. Drizzle the cake with 2 tablespoons cream sherry, then pour over 400 ml (14 fl oz) good-quality ready-made fresh custard. Top with spoonfuls of crème fraîche. Decorate with fresh strawberry quarters.

Plum Compote, Marzipan and Madeira Pudding Melt 25 g (1 oz) butter in a heavy-based saucepan and cook 6 plums, stoned and cut into chunks, over a medium heat, stirring occasionally, for 2 minutes. Add 50 g (2 oz) caster sugar, ½ teaspoon ground cinnamon and 1 tablespoon water and cook, stirring occasionally, for a further 2 minutes until the plums are tender. Place in the bottom of a large, shallow gratin dish. Cover with 4 thick slices of Madeira cake, then top with 175 g (6 oz) grated marzipan. Place in the top of a preheated oven, 190°C (375°F), Gas Mark 5, for 15 minutes until the marzipan is browned in places.

Treacle Sponge Microwave Puddings

Serves 4

100 g (3½ oz) butter, softened, plus extra for greasing

100 g (3½ oz) soft light brown sugar

100 g (3½ oz) self-raising flour

1 teaspoon mixed spice

1 egg, beaten

4 tablespoons golden syrup

custard, to serve

- Lightly grease 4 x 150 ml (¼ pint) ramekins and line the bases with baking parchment. Beat the butter with the sugar in a bowl until pale and fluffy, then sift in the flour and spice and add the egg. Beat together until well mixed.

- Divide the mixture between the prepared ramekins. Cover each with a disc of baking parchment and cook together in a microwave oven on high for 2–2½ minutes, then leave the sponges to rest for 3–4 minutes to finish cooking.

- Turn each pudding out on to a serving plate and drizzle each with 1 tablespoon of the golden syrup while still warm. Serve with custard.

 Warm Treacle Madeira Cake

Cut 1 shop-bought Madeira cake into chunks and place in the base of an ovenproof dish. Place 5 tablespoons golden syrup in a saucepan with 25 g (1 oz) butter and 2 tablespoons soft light brown sugar. Heat gently, stirring constantly, for 2 minutes until the syrup is warm and well blended with the butter. Pour over the cake cubes and heat in a microwave oven on high for 1 minute. Serve warm with scoops of ice cream.

 Baked Treacle Sponge

Grease a 1 litre (1¾ pint) shallow baking dish and spoon in 6 tablespoons golden syrup. In a food processor, whizz together 100 g (3½ oz) each softened butter and caster sugar, 2 beaten eggs and 1 teaspoon vanilla extract. Add 100 g (3½ oz) self-raising flour and pulse until just mixed. Scrape into the baking dish and place in a preheated oven, 180°C (350°F), Gas Mark 4, for 25 minutes until golden. Serve with hot shop-bought ready-made custard.

30 Chocolate Puddle Pudding

Serves 4

75 g (3 oz) unsalted butter, softened
75 g (3 oz) soft light brown sugar
3 eggs
65 g (2½ oz) self-raising flour
3 tablespoons cocoa powder
½ teaspoon baking powder
icing sugar, for dusting
ice cream or cream, to serve

For the sauce

2 tablespoons cocoa powder
50 g (2 oz) soft light brown sugar
250 ml (8 fl oz) boiling water

- Grease a 600 ml (1 pint) gratin dish with a little of the butter. Place the remaining butter, brown sugar and eggs in a large bowl and sift in the flour, cocoa and baking powder. Beat together until smooth. Spoon the mixture into the prepared dish and spread the top level.

- For the sauce, place the cocoa and sugar in a bowl and mix in a little of the measurement water to make a smooth paste, then add the remaining water, a little at a time, and mix until smooth.

- Pour the sauce over the pudding mixture and place in a preheated oven, 200°C (400°F), Gas Mark 6, for 15 minutes or until the sauce has sunk to the bottom of the dish and the pudding is well risen. Dust with icing sugar and serve with ice cream or cream.

 Chocolate Sponges with Hot Chocolate Sauce Heat 4 shop-bought chocolate sponge cakes or muffins in a microwave for 1 minute until warmed through. Meanwhile, mix 1 teaspoon finely grated orange rind into 115 g (3½ oz) clotted cream. Make the chocolate sauce as above. Serve the warm cakes or muffins covered with the hot sauce and topped with a spoonful of the orange cream.

 Chocolate Pancakes with Hot Chocolate Sauce In a food processor, whizz together 100 g (3½ oz) plain flour, 1 tablespoon cocoa powder, 1 egg and 200 ml (7 fl oz) milk until smooth. Heat a little vegetable oil in a nonstick frying pan and cook the pancakes in batches, using 100 ml (3½ fl oz) batter at a time, over a medium–high heat for 1–2 minutes. Flip and cook on the other side. Remove and keep warm. Make the chocolate sauce as above. Serve the pancakes drizzled with the hot sauce, dusted with icing sugar and with ice cream on the side.

Caramel Pear Tarte Tatin

Serves 4–6

butter, for greasing
2 x 400 g (13 oz) cans pears in
    fruit juice, drained
5 tablespoons dulce de leche
375 g (12 oz) pack ready-made
    sweet shortcrust pastry,
    defrosted if frozen
plain flour, for dusting
ice cream or cream, to serve

· Line the base of a 23 cm (9 inch) loose-bottomed cake tin with baking parchment and grease.

· Place the pears and dulce de leche in a saucepan and heat over a gentle heat for 1–2 minutes, stirring occasionally, until the pears are well coated in the sauce. Arrange the pears in the base of the prepared tin in a single layer.

· Roll out the pastry on a lightly floured work surface to a circle slightly larger than the tin and place over the pears, folding any surplus up the side of the tin.

· Place in a preheated oven, 220°C (425°F), Gas Mark 7, for 20 minutes until the pastry is golden and cooked. Run a knife around the edge of the tart and turn out on to a serving plate. Serve cut into wedges with ice cream or cream.

---

1 Pan-Fried Caramelized Pears

Melt 25 g (1 oz) butter in a large, heavy-based frying pan. Take 2 x 400 g (13 oz) cans pears in fruit juice, drain and quarter the pears and place in a bowl. Coat the pears in 5 tablespoons dulce de leche, then fry until the sauce is bubbling and the pears are softened. Serve with scoops of ice cream, drizzled with caramel or toffee sauce.

2 Individual Caramel Pear Tarts

Cut out 4 x 10 cm (4 inch) circles, using a small dish or saucer as a guide, from a 375 g (12 oz) pack ready-rolled shortcrust pastry and place on a baking sheet. Prick all over with a fork, then place in a preheated oven, 200°C (400°F), Gas Mark 6, for 10 minutes until golden. Meanwhile, drain a 400 g (13 oz) can pears in fruit juice and roughly chop or slice. Melt 25 g (1 oz) butter in a saucepan and cook the pears over a medium-high heat, stirring frequently, for 2 minutes, then sprinkle over 3 tablespoons soft dark brown sugar and cook, tossing, for a further 1 minute. Add 2 tablespoons double cream and stir well to make a caramel sauce. Spoon the caramel pears over the pastry discs on serving plates and serve with ice cream, if liked.

10 Scone, Strawberry and Clotted Cream Trifles

Serves 4

175 g (6 oz) fresh strawberries, hulled and quartered, plus 2 extra, halved, to decorate
4 tablespoons strawberry jam
4 tablespoons clotted cream
2 shop-bought plain scones, halved

- Place the strawberries in a bowl and mix with the strawberry jam. Divide half the strawberries between the bases of 4 serving glasses and top each with a spoonful of the cream and then a scone half.

- Spoon over the remaining strawberries, then decorate each trifle with a strawberry half.

2 Scone and Berry Boozy Trifle

Place 250 g (8 oz) fresh hulled strawberries, 125 g (4 oz) fresh raspberries and 4 tablespoons strawberry or raspberry conserve in a bowl. Mix well, then transfer to a trifle bowl. Roughly chop 4 shop-bought plain scones and scatter over the top, then drizzle with 6 tablespoons dry sherry. Pour over 600 ml (1 pint) chilled shop-bought ready-made vanilla custard and then spoon over 400 ml (13 fl oz) crème fraîche. Decorate with halved strawberries, if liked.

3 Mixed Berry Compote and

Scone Bake Place 500 g (1 lb) frozen mixed summer berries in a saucepan with 125 g (4 oz) caster sugar and 4 tablespoons dry sherry or water. Bring to the boil, then pour into a large, shallow gratin dish. Halve 4 plain scones and arrange, cut-side down, over the compote. Sprinkle with 5 tablespoons demerara sugar mixed with ½ teaspoon ground cinnamon. Place in a preheated oven, 190°C (375°F), Gas Mark 5, for 15 minutes. Serve with custard.

Speedy Apple Crumble-Style Desserts

Serves 4

25 g (1 oz) unsalted butter
2 large Bramley cooking apples, peeled, cored and cut into chunks
4 tablespoons soft dark brown sugar
4 tablespoons double cream
8 tablespoons granola crunchy oat cereal
2 tablespoons toasted flaked almonds
clotted cream, to serve (optional)

- Melt the butter in a heavy-based frying pan and cook the apple chunks over a medium heat, stirring occasionally, for 5–6 minutes until tender and browned.

- Add the sugar and cook, stirring, for 1 minute. Add the cream and cook, stirring, for a further 1 minute until the sauce is caramel coloured and the apples are tender yet still retaining their shape.

- Divide the apple mixture between 4 warmed serving bowls. Mix the oat cereal with the almonds and spoon over the top of the hot apple mixture. Serve with a spoonful of clotted cream on top, if liked.

Apple and Raspberry Grilled Crumbles

Mix a 400 g (13 oz) can or jar prepared apples or apple pie filling with 100 g (3½ oz) fresh raspberries and divide between 4 individual ramekins. Top with 8 tablespoons granola crunch cereal mixed with 2 tablespoons ground almonds. Dot with butter and cook under a preheated medium grill for 2 minutes until warm. Serve with vanilla ice cream.

Flapjack-Style Summer Fruit Crumble

Place 500 g (1 lb) frozen mixed summer fruits in a baking dish and sprinkle over 4 tablespoons caster sugar. Melt 100 g (3½ oz) butter and 100 g (3½ oz) golden syrup in a saucepan and stir in 150 g (5 oz) porridge oats and 20 g (¾ oz) ground almonds. Spread the mixture over the fruit and place in a preheated oven, 180°C (350°F), Gas Mark 4, for 25 minutes until golden. Serve with good-quality vanilla ice cream.

3 Meringue-Topped Tangy Lemon Cups

Serves 4

finely grated rind and juice
  of 2 lemons
150 g (5 oz) caster sugar
2 tablespoons cornflour
1 egg yolk
2 egg whites
1 teaspoon soft light brown sugar

- Place the lemon rind and juice in a small saucepan with 75 g (3 oz) of the caster sugar and 150 ml (¼ pint) water. Bring to the boil. Meanwhile, blend 3 tablespoons water into the cornflour in a heatproof bowl, pour over the hot liquid, stirring constantly, and mix well until thickened. Stir in the egg yolk. Return to the pan and cook, stirring constantly, for 1 minute until thickened. Divide between 4 individual ramekins or gratin dishes.

- Whisk the egg whites in a grease-free bowl until stiff. Add 1 tablespoon of the remaining caster sugar at a time, whisking well between each addition, until the meringue is smooth and glossy.

- Spoon the meringue mixture over the lemon cups and sprinkle with the brown sugar. Place the dishes on a baking sheet and cook under a preheated high grill for 1–2 minutes until the tops are lightly golden and have firmed a little. Serve warm.

---

1 Tangy Lemon Eton Mess

Break 8 shop-bought meringue nests into small chunks and place in a bowl. Whip 300 ml (½ pint) double cream in a separate bowl until thick and mix into the meringue, followed by 200 g (7 oz) hulled and halved strawberries and 1 teaspoon finely grated lemon rind. Serve in individual glass bowls garnished with mint sprigs.

2 Tangy Lemon Curd Puddings

In a food processor, whizz together 125 g (4 oz) each softened butter, caster sugar and self-raising flour, 2 beaten eggs and the finely grated rind of 1 lemon until well blended. Drop 1 tablespoon shop-bought lemon curd into the base of 4 individual greased ramekins. Spoon the sponge mixture on top, cover with clingfilm and cook in a microwave oven individually on high for 1½ minutes until risen and cooked through. Leave to rest for 1 minute before serving with vanilla ice cream.

 # Caramel Bananas

Serves 4

25 g (1 oz) butter
50 g (2 oz) soft light brown sugar
4 bananas, peeled
8 tablespoons double cream
vanilla ice cream, to serve

- Melt the butter in a large, heavy-based frying pan, add the sugar and heat gently until the sugar has dissolved and the butter is foaming.

- Cut the bananas in half lengthways, then cut each half in half again widthways. Add to the pan and cook over a medium heat, stirring and turning gently once or twice, for 3–4 minutes until softened. Remove with a fish slice and divide between 4 warmed serving bowls.

- Add the cream to the pan and stir well with a wooden spoon. Spoon the sauce over the bananas and serve with scoops of vanilla ice cream.

 Rum and Raisin Banana Pancakes
Make up a 150 g (5 oz) packet batter mix according to the packet instructions. Melt 25 g (1 oz) butter in a large, heavy-based frying pan, add 50 g (2 oz) soft light brown sugar and heat gently until the sugar has dissolved and the butter is foaming. Cut 4 peeled bananas in half lengthways, then each half in half again widthways. Add to the pan and cook over a medium heat, stirring and turning gently once or twice, for 2–3 minutes. Add 4 tablespoons raisins and cook for a further 1 minute, then add 2 tablespoons dark rum and set alight. Remove from the heat and allow the flames to die down. Heat a lightly greased 23 cm (9 inch) nonstick frying pan and cook the batter in 4 batches over a medium-high heat for 30 seconds–1 minute on each side until golden. Fill the pancakes with the bananas and serve warm, with ice cream, if liked.

Baked Bananas with Chocolate and Honey Lay 4 unpeeled ripe bananas in a roasting tin and place in a preheated oven, 200°C (400°F), Gas Mark 6, for 20 minutes until blackened and very soft. Remove from the oven, make a slit down the skin of each and drizzle with clear honey. Scatter with 50 g (2 oz) roughly chopped plain dark chocolate and serve with spoonfuls of crème fraîche or ice cream.

Quick Tiramisu with Strawberries

Serves 4–6

150 ml (¼ pint) strong coffee, cooled

75 g (3 oz) soft light brown sugar

4 tablespoons coffee liqueur

100 g (3½ oz) sponge fingers, snapped in half

300 ml (½ pint) shop-bought ready-made fresh custard

250 g (8 oz) mascarpone cheese

1 teaspoon vanilla extract

125 g (4 oz) plain dark chocolate, roughly chopped

125 g (4 oz) fresh strawberries, hulled and thinly sliced

cocoa powder, for dusting

- Place the coffee, sugar and liqueur in a large bowl. Add the sponge fingers and gently toss to soak in the mixture, then transfer to a shallow serving dish, spooning over any excess liquid.

- Beat the custard with the mascarpone and vanilla extract in a separate bowl, then spoon half over the soaked biscuits and spread evenly. Scatter half the chocolate over the top followed by the strawberries.

- Spoon the remaining mascarpone mixture over the strawberries and spread evenly. Scatter over the remaining chocolate and dust with cocoa. Chill until ready to serve.

 Irish Cream Liqueur Tiramisu

Press 8 halved sponge fingers into 4 glass serving dishes. Pour over enough cold coffee to soak the sponges. Sprinkle 1 tablespoon Irish cream liqueur over each dish, then top each with 1 scoop Irish cream liqueur ice cream, 1 tablespoon softly whipped cream and a sprinkling of grated plain dark chocolate. Serve immediately.

 Tiramisu-Style Cheesecake

Place 200 g (7 oz) amaretti biscuits in a polythene bag and bash with a rolling pin to form fine crumbs. Mix with 50 g (2 oz) melted butter and press into an 18 cm (7 inch) loose-bottomed cake tin. Refrigerate for a few minutes. Dissolve 1 tablespoon instant coffee in 4 tablespoons hot water and 2 tablespoons brandy in a large bowl. Briefly dip 10 sponge fingers in the mixture and set aside. Beat 500 g (1 lb) mascarpone cheese with 40 g (1½ oz) icing sugar and spread half over the chilled biscuit base. Lay the sponge fingers on top and top with the remaining mascarpone mixture. Chill until required and dust with cocoa powder before serving. Serve with fresh summer berries, if liked.

Index

Page references in *italics* indicate photographs

Acknowledgements

Recipes by Emma Jane Frost
Executive Editor Eleanor Maxfield
Senior Editor Sybella Stephens
Copy Editor Jo Richardson
Art Direction Mark Kan
Design www.gradedesign.com
Photographer Stephen Conroy
Home Economist Emma Jane Frost
Prop Stylist Isabel De Cordova
Production Peter Hunt